SUBVERSIVE

Interviews with Radicals

Brian Whitney

Headpress

Introduction

When I first thought of this book it was to be different. This was to be a book of interviews with people who do, or have done, things that society finds abhorrent or possibly ridiculous, but that could literally care less about what others think. Many people talk the talk about living life their own way despite societal pressures, but how many people actually do it? How many people have the resolve to live in a way that puts them in the way of scorn, ridicule, or possibly even danger?

I fell into the habit of seeking such people out for a website I was writing for, and thought a book of such pieces would be an interesting document. I had interviewed a writer who used heroin and didn't want to stop, I talked to pedophiles that chose not to act on their sexual urges, I interviewed a man who was a confidant of the Unabomber, another man who claimed he could make people immortal, and also a member of the Flat Earth Society. And the thing is, with each published interview, readers tended to get so fucking mad. Not all people of course, but enough to pique my interest. Scores of people would comment on these pieces, and either mock the subject, or wish the person dead.

This intrigued me. Why does someone get angry with someone who shoots up heroin and is proud of it? Why does one want to kill a man who is attracted to children and has never acted on it? Why do people care so much about what other people think about immortality or the shape of the Earth?

Why do we always need to be right? Why do other people have to live the same way we do?

I am not enlightened. I don't have a philosophy. I am not one to spend his days trying to change society. That would be something to be proud of, I suppose. But that isn't it. I simply just don't care what others do. For example, it isn't that I am pro gay rights, it is more that I simply don't care if you stick your cock up another guy's ass. I don't care what you do really. I do think it is not so nice to murder someone, or to steal, but really if you do such things does it really change anything? Does it really make you wrong?

These were the questions I wanted to ask. I wanted to find people all over the world who had done things or are actively doing things that society thinks are oh so wrong, and I wanted to know why they didn't care.

While this was a noble cause, or at least I like to think so, in time the focus of the book shifted. I found that there was no way I would be able to find enough people to talk to me under those parameters to complete a book of interviews. My elevator pitch was way off. It was kind of like "Hey, I am doing a book where I interview people who do things that society thinks are fucked up, but they don't care. Want to be in it?" Not surprisingly that did not intrigue a lot of people. I searched high and low for unrepentant con men, thieves, murderers, druggies and drunks, but I was striking out left and right.

So I went slightly more towards the middle. I decided to try and find subversives. When it comes down to it, there is not much of a shift here as one might think, they are still people that are doing things, or have done them, that most of society finds completely wrong, or ridiculous, but there are just so many more people in this pool that wanted to talk to me than in the previous one.

One usually thinks of a subversive as being a political sort, who is trying to undermine the current system. There are many of those types in this book. There are also many subversives or other types here as well; the ones that subvert current sexual, societal and moral mores are here too.

Of course, I am one of these people myself, and it was not much of a jump to find people that thought like me, that did their own thing and did it either to tear down society, or because they simply did not care at all what society thought of them.

Where before it seemed to the interviewee that I was trying to take advantage of them and maybe even mock them, now it became apparent to all that I was one of them. It took me just a few months to line up some of the most radical people in the world to do interviews with me. Don't get me wrong. A lot of people told me to fuck off, and the Unabomber wrote me back to decline and told me that I had some of the worst handwriting he had ever seen.

The people that were kind enough to talk to me are anarchists, socialists and primitivists. They are unrepentant drug users, they are people that have been put in prison for their sexual tendencies, and they are authors of books on how to make meth and nerve gas. They are murderers, they are imposters, they are white nationalists, and they are Black Panthers. They are 9-11 Truthers, they are occultists, and they worship gods from outer space. They are antinatalists, sexual deviants, and men's activists.

Some of them are well-known and have a large following, others are known by few, or mocked by many.

All of them are brave and all of them think for themselves.

Do your own thing. It is way easier in the long run. Unless of course your thing is doing something illegal. Then you are probably fucked either way.

"...eternal life is impossible and anything that's not eternal will inevitably seem too short when it's finally over."

Shane Levene

While most people think of heroin users as a bunch of hapless addicts, a lot of people that use don't want to quit. This goes far beyond the "just try and use less" world of harm reduction. Many people that use heroin simply can't imagine life without it, they just want to use and be left alone. One of these people is the ridiculously talented poet and writer SHANE LEVENE. You can find his writing on his website, entitled Memoires of a Heroinhead.

Many people can't imagine trying heroin under any circumstances. What do you think separates those that use from those that don't? Where were you at mentally and emotionally when you first shot up?

For those many people who cannot envisage using heroin under any circumstance then they've certainly not thought too hard over what heroin is, where else it is used, or what extreme or unfortunate circumstances can lead to someone having to use it. The uncontrolled heroin which is sold on the street is only the sharp point of the needle. A lot of the heroin circulating in our society is a strictly controlled, legal substance and is arguably the single most important drug that hospitals and doctors have to treat severe and long term pain. People hear the word heroin, flip out, and in that neurosis remain in such ignorance that it comes as a huge surprise to learn that this same drug is used to treat valid ailments as varied as arthritis, spinal injuries and cancer. The only difference is that in hospitals it is called diamorphine. So, for those people who cannot imagine ever using heroin then they had better hope that they are never in a serious traffic accident, or fall off a horse, damage their spine or come down with a terminal condition. I guarantee they'd change their tune then and wouldn't be so Jehovah about it. In comparison to the pain, heroin would quickly seem like quite an attractive offer. That attraction is no less alluring when dealing with emotional pain or trauma and turning to the heroin that is sold on the street. But such are the kind of people above that they will never concede a point and would argue to the death that taking heroin when it is prescribed is in no way comparable to those who purchase it illicitly and self-medicate. I'd be interested to see their expressions on learning of the proportion of heroin addicts who began buying on the street after picking up an initial habit through prescribed opiates.

But what it all really goes to show is how heroin is viewed by the general populace, how the anti-heroin propaganda (like all great propaganda) ensures people remain ignorant and one-dimensional in their knowledge and thoughts. Still, with that said, I don't doubt for a moment that such people will never go and score heroin on the street. The point is that the street is not the only place where heroin is found and used or misused. The legal opiate market is substantial, and the truth is that the illegal heroin trade (as rampant as it is) is only possible on the back of the legal industry, very often the two combine and are quite indistinguishable from each other.

What separates those who use and those who don't (and I refer now only to illegal street heroin) is a quite unfathomable mix of components. In fact, if anyone knew the answer to that question then we probably wouldn't have the heroin epidemic that we currently do. You will read online and in pseudoscientific studies of common factors often found in the demographic of heroin users. But regardless of how specific those factors are, or how astute people are in their observations, it is always the case that still most people who have those qualities do not become addicts. So much comes down to chance and psychology (and psychology is a very hazardous thing in itself) that there really isn't a very accurate profile of someone who is likely to become an addict. It's probably easier to predict who will certainly not become an addict, but as that is most people then it's no real insight anyway.

I once talked to Shilo Murphy, who is one of the founders of the Drug User's Union and he said "Heroin saved my life." Can you relate to that at all? Has heroin saved you?
Well, as I always say: heroin kills me as it cures me. But that was always the deal. Without beginning to use heroin at that period in my life I would never have survived. Life had become too irritating and my skin was down to the raw. Heroin numbed the pain enough to make it bearable, just. But, contrary to what many say, heroin is not this drug that numbs you beyond all feeling. That's bullshit. People still feel and hurt and suffer and cry on heroin but the pain is subdued enough to make it bearable, to allow one to persevere even while carrying the burden of their trauma. So heroin, though the effects of it will eventually be a factor in my death, allowed me to live through years I'd never have survived without it. I accept that. It still seems like a good deal. It would have been even better had I not had to make such a deal but that's a useless exercise to get into as what has happened stays happened. Under

the exact same circumstances, knowing all I know today, I'd still make the same decision.

Do you ever think about quitting? Society thinks you should.
Society never thinks, that's the problem. Society is swayed and prodded and subtly pushed and encouraged in certain directions by certain people with even more certain agendas. So I don't really give a fuck about what society thinks it thinks or knows. Society reflects the views of all the people and philosophies I am opposed to. Society, if viewed as an organism, would be just about the most stupid, easily manipulated and blinkered piece of crap alive. So, no, I NEVER contemplate quitting heroin in the way that society and the society riddled rehabs and drug groups would ever accept. I use heroin and I will use it when and how I choose. That doesn't mean I may never stop but it does mean I will never vow to quit and stay quit. This philosophy of total and absolute abstinence, of punishment and retribution for those who 'fuck up' is more damaging and unhealthy than anything. It immediately creates temptation in people's lives, resides like a permanent reminder inside their heads and debases and humiliates then. It also instantly pits you against the helpers and doctors, those very people who are supposed to have your best interests at heart. What exists at the moment is an authoritarian system of care based upon the threat of retribution. And yet it can only end in retribution because the criterion for success is so unrealistic. We need a complete rethink over what success could be in treating drug addiction and what we want from users in treatment, regardless of whether they use or not.

So, I have periods where I do not use but I only ever go into that saying, "I'm having a break," and I never attach any kind of time to that. It could be one day or one month, a year or maybe, if I feel it and it comes naturally, forever. But if ever I feel like using in those times I will. I'll use and then not use again tomorrow. I'll not beat myself up over it, nor feel guilty, nor damn myself as a 'fuck up' or a letdown. That is a much healthier way of treating addiction and it also gives the bodies that be a genuine insight into addiction and usage patterns. But the moment punishment is doled out, in any system, it only ever leads to dishonest interaction and a false exchange of information.

As a writer do you find that heroin helps you be more creative or does it bog you down?
As a writer and artist I feel that creativity cannot be conditional upon being stoned. If it is, then shame on that person who is masquerading as either. Creativity must be a poison secreted by the soul. If you are not poisoned by creativity then no drug and no experience can help you. The artist must be an artist at all times. If life and the fatalistic journey towards death isn't enough to

pull something great from someone then no amount of drugs can give them that. All drugs can do is give an already creative person a focus point, an extreme experience or event which they can then direct their creative energies towards. Me, personally, I very rarely write while on heroin. It's a physical thing. I just don't stay conscious long enough to get anything down. Mentally my mind works just as well but the effects of heroin just aren't compatible with an art form that requires one to sit down and concentrate for long periods.

What about death, we all know that people can die from using heroin, does that freak you out?
Death freaks me out, period. Too much in this world kills us. Junk food; smoking; breathing; mining; sunbathing; alcohol; sex; stupidity. If we avoided everything that could be potentially fatal we'd not move a muscle and our lives would be pretty dull and not much worth living anyway. I don't want to die by heroin nor by any other means. My lifestyle may seem to contradict that—I inject heroin, chain-smoke, eat terribly and take air from the polluted city—but that's only because eternal life is impossible and anything that's not eternal will inevitably seem too short when it's finally over. So I do what I do for as long as I can and that's so much better than doing nothing at all for a little longer. And like that I have a hand in my own death and destiny and there's nothing more empowering than that.

Gil Valle

GIL VALLE is the Cannibal Cop. He used to be a member of New York City's finest, until his wife caught him messing around on a website called Dark Fetish Network, where Gil and other users spent their evenings fantasizing about how they wanted to kidnap and eat a whole bunch of women. Being cooked and eaten freaked her out and she went to the FBI. Despite no evidence of any real world criminal activities, Gil was arrested and eventually sentenced to fifteen years in prison for conspiracy to kidnap. After he served twenty-one months or so, a judge overturned the sentence and he was exonerated. Gil's memoir, *Raw Deal*, will be released in 2017.

How did you first come to find Dark Fetish Network, and how often did you use it?

I came across DFN through one of those "related sites" kind of things around September 2009. I don't remember what website I was looking at; it was probably something to do with BDSM porn. I began to browse DFN and found that it was sort of like a social media site for people with unusual sexual fantasies. This place runs the whole spectrum as far as fetishes go; Bondage, cannibalism/vore, torture, castration, pissing, shitting, slavery, leather, executions, mummification, and on and on. Most of the stuff did not appeal to me but it seemed that there was something there for everyone with an unusual sexual fetish.

I became intrigued when I was browsing photo albums and saw that some members of the site were posing pictures of ordinary women that they said they knew. It looked like the pictures were hijacked from Facebook pages. The consistent theme was "What Would You Do With Her?" and people would leave comments tailored towards their sexual fetishes.

I had an interest in bondage porn throughout my puberty years but I became interested in cannibal related porn sometime in college when I discovered a website called Muki's Kitchen. What I would do, whether or not it was BDSM or cannibalism related, was read stories or look at pictures and if I liked them,

"I wouldn't go driving around, seeing a hot woman and thinking to myself, 'Wow, she'd look great tied up.'"

I would imagine women I knew in my life in those situations.

So when I saw what was going on with DFN, I decided to create an account and participate. I created a profile with the user name "Girlmeat Hunter" and indicated that I was interested in fantasies involving kidnapping, bondage, and cannibalism. My fantasies and scenarios involved non-consensual victims. Others enjoyed fantasies involving women who would consent to being tortured, hung, eaten, or whatever. The consensual scenarios didn't appeal to me. I noticed that the website hammered home the fact that this was all fantasy only, so I echoed that in my profile just to be safe. I know I would never hurt anyone despite enjoying graphic, brutal scenarios involving women I know, but I thought it was good just to put that disclaimer in my profile just to be sure.

I created my very own "What Would You Do" album. I had Facebook pictures from about ten women I knew downloaded, and I posted them in the album. I didn't use names at first. It was Girl #1, Girl #2, etc. I remember this being early on a Friday morning because I was going to travel down to Maryland for a football game at the university for the weekend. When I was finished posting the pictures, I packed up and left for Maryland.

When I came back Sunday night, I logged back into DFN and saw that I had around fifty comments from other users regarding the photos. People were giving their ideas and their scenarios for what they would do with the women who I posted. They were mostly bondage and cannibal related comments. I came to realize that was kind of a rule of the site; you would read the user's profile and leave comments related to that person's sexual fetishes. I read all of the comments for each of the ten or so women I posted and I remember thinking some of them were interesting and detailed. If I liked them, I would incorporate them into my scenarios when I masturbated.

That's how it all started. I got a lot of positive feedback and I liked a lot of the ideas from other users, so I posted more and more women. Towards the beginning of all of this, I was still living at home with my father. I was three years into my police career. I would usually log on to DFN after I got home from work around one in the morning, in addition to checking my email, Facebook, news, etc. When things were getting more serious with my girlfriend, who later became my wife, it was a lot less frequent.

What kind of chats were you and your buddy engaged in? Was it mostly the kidnap and eat kind of thing or was it all over the board?
In addition to the comments people left on the photos, I was starting to get direct messages from other users. They would usually pick out one of the women I posted and asked if I wanted to do a role-play centering on her. Again, these messages were from people who experienced similar sexual fantasies.

I wouldn't get messages about one of the photos from someone who was into mummification, for instance. I would sometimes get messages from users who said they were women, and they wanted to do a role-play/story where I was the captor and they were the victim but I was not into that. I enjoyed role-playing the scenarios involving the women I knew. I discovered that the fact that I knew the women kind of enhanced the stories for me. As we got into the role-plays, I was able to envision how the woman would sound as she was gagged, and so on.

I appreciated and enjoyed detailed role-plays the most. I am well educated, and I liked when other users were able to write well. The general theme of all of the role-plays was kidnapping and bondage. If I liked the way the other user wrote, sometimes we would tailor the story towards what he or she was interested in. Some of the people I chatted with were more into blood, gore, and torture, which generally didn't turn me on. Other people enjoyed a slavery scenario, where the kidnapped woman would be put up for auction and sold to the highest bidder. I started to enjoy that theme more and more so I began to incorporate it. When I created new albums, I would title them "Cook Her or Sell Her?"

As long as the role-play involved some kind of kidnapping and bondage, I was generally okay with it. The good role-plays I would incorporate into my masturbatory sessions. As far as the cannibalism part of it, I never got to the part where I was actually eating the person. The idea of the girl tied up and being prepared to be cooked was the peak of it. As I said before, I am not turned on by the blood and gore side of things.

Did you ever think, the whole time when you were together with your wife, that you could maybe tell her the kind of thing that you were into? Or did you just assume she would freak out?
The idea of telling my girlfriend/wife about all of this never entered my mind. I thought it was way too taboo, and I thought she would run away from me! *Fifty Shades [of Grey]* hadn't come out when we started dating. I was fine with the conventional sex. I was often so caught up in the pleasure of the moment, I rarely ever thought about the fantasies. On occasion, though, I would imagine her tied to the bed but that was about it.

During the summer of 2012, I left the computer we were sharing open and she saw one of the bondage porn sites I was looking at. It wasn't DFN, but she confronted me about it. I was really embarrassed and nervous and I fumbled to explain myself. I basically told her the truth. Sometimes I would come home from work, she and the baby were sleeping, not much to do, so I'd look at pornography and I was always into bondage websites. To my surprise, she said she was willing to try some light bondage. I was really excited about the idea. Later that day, she had texted me the location of some sex shop in Manhattan.

Out of embarrassment I think, I never went to the sex shop. This was around August, and only two weeks later the installed the spyware and found the DFN stuff that frightened her and resulted in her wanting to get away for a while. She didn't just pack up and run away immediately like the FBI and the media made it seem. She woke me up and we talked about it. She said she was freaked out by what she saw and she just wanted some time away with her parents. She was in the apartment with me for about three hours before she left. I fed the baby and played with her while Kathleen was showering, packing, and getting ready. Law enforcement's account was that she found the website and left with nothing but the baby and the clothes on her back. Not true.

Her initial reaction, later that day, was that we were going to get through this. She suggested that I find a couples' therapist and we will work this out when she comes back. I have all of the text messages between us from that time period and they are very difficult for me to read and re-live that.

Did it ever occur to you, as you were engaging your fantasies, that what you were doing could have been considered illegal by anyone?
In my worst nightmare, I could have never imagined what ended up happening. Like I said, I enjoyed role-plays that were detailed and sounded real, but I made clear in my DFN profile that no matter what I say it's all just fantasies. The way the prosecution worked out, I wish I would have made that disclaimer in every set of chats I engaged in. They prosecuted me for chats where that disclaimer was never made, but nonetheless, I thought it was crystal clear that these were not real plans. There were a couple of chats where me and the other participant talked about doing it for real, but that was done to enhance the story. Constantly making the fantasy disclaimer would kind of take the air out of the balloon. Despite the "real" talk, the surrounding circumstances clearly show that these, though they sounded real, were still just stories.

For one, there was never any personal information exchanged between me and anyone I was chatting with. No names, addresses, phone numbers, etc. The only communication was through screen names and our real identities were not shared. Also, weeks and sometimes months would pass between chats with certain users. When the chats resumed, they often started over (new "victim", new scenario).

Moreover, the details I provided about who I was and my location were all false. In my role-plays, I was a character who had a van and a mountain house in the middle of nowhere. Of course, in reality, none of that existed.

I was aware that the practice of taking women's Facebook pictures and posting them on a website without their consent was completely unethical, but it certainly was not criminal. During role-plays, I would provide the woman's first name, sometimes her occupation and age, but I was careful not to provide anything that would enable someone to locate them. It wasn't that I was concerned that someone I was chatting with would try and look these women up and harm them, I just wanted to protect the women's identities. I used their photos and some circumstances of their lives to create fictional characters, just like me and my role-play partner were.

I didn't enjoy comic book type stuff. I chatted with a lot of people through DFN, but the ones that I enjoyed and went back to were ones that were graphic, detailed, and sounded real. People don't have to like that but it is clear—now that the case is over and I won everything—that nothing I did was criminal.

For someone, like my wife, who was completely unaware what was going on to stumble on this stuff, I totally understand her and anyone else being really freaked out. The language and acts surrounding these stories were incredibly violent and being an anonymous avatar on the other side of a computer screen kind of allows you to go a little crazy. You kind of try and outdo the other person. "Ok that was pretty sick, but I can do better" kind of mindset.

I could always empathize with her wanting to talk to law enforcement about what she saw. But once the FBI got involved, it should have been pretty transparent that all of this stuff was fake. They even put a tracker on my phone and knew my exact location for thirty straight days. All they saw was me going to and from work. Their paperwork asking a judge for the warrant to track my phone indicated that they expected that tracking me would lead to evidence of the kidnapping conspiracy. I think they were looking for the mountain house that didn't exist.

Still, it got to the point of them arresting me. I can understand the investigation, but arresting me was an absolute joke. To compound matters, the FBI and prosecutors often misrepresented facts early on in the case. A lot of it was clearly intentional. They lied about GPS tracking evidence they claimed they had, they lied about me working on days when they knew I was off, they lied about the details of my friendship with the girl from Maryland. It goes on and on. My fantasies don't hold a candle to their fantasy of wanting to make me out to be a real criminal.

Of course, once the trial started, they abandoned many of their earlier claims. People told me that if you black out my name from the court transcripts and you read the bail/preliminary hearings and the trial, you would think they are two completely separate cases.

For the judge to do what he did—overturn the jury's verdict AND dismiss the charge—(and for that ruling to be upheld), you not only know that what I did was not criminal but if you go through the case with a lens from a legal perspective, you'd easily conclude that there was rampant prosecutorial misconduct as well as perjury committed by an FBI agent. Sadly, to this point, although perjury is a crime (the only crime committed in this case), and it is clear that the perjury was proven, nobody gives a damn. Hopefully that will change.

It seems that those who have somewhat unusual fantasies in our society are often deeply ashamed of them. Do you think your situation offers people with similar fantasies hope for acceptance, or drives them further underground?

To this point, I think what happened to me would drive people further underground. I've read a lot of paperwork about my case, including briefings from psychologists who are familiar with sexual fantasies. It seems that many people do have sexual fantasies and taboo interests that they would never share with anyone. Most of the people, like me, are able to just live with them. Though I was engaged in fictional role-plays, once the computer was off I was back to being me. I wouldn't go driving around, seeing a hot woman and thinking to myself, "Wow, she'd look great tied up."

I was living a very successful life. I had passed the NYPD sergeant's exam, I was married with a kid, making good money and I had lived with having sexual fantasies about kidnapping and bondage since my teenage years. I never once had an impulse or an urge to act on those and I never would.

For me to do as well as I was doing and to have everything blow up in my face despite not breaking any laws, I think people who are in similar situations would be more reluctant to share any of their taboo interests with people, let alone having their deepest, darkest secrets being broadcast in front of the entire world. I would not wish what happened to me on my worst enemy.

However, I think in the last handful of years there has been more of an acceptance and understanding of the whole BDSM realm. I think Fifty Shades had something to do with that, but I haven't really studied it enough. I am also aware that there are clubs and websites such as Alt.com that cater towards people with unusual fetishes. I think there are different degrees too. Someone who enjoys light bondage would be much more likely to share that than someone who has more violent fantasies.

For me, there is some good with the fact that all of this is now out there. I have had women find me on Facebook and not only offer all kinds of encouragement, but they also say that they are turned on by my fantasies and have fantasies themselves of being tied up and raped. It's kind of surreal sometimes. I do want to start dating again and one of the big questions I have for people is, at what point do I tell a woman about the fact that I was arrested and known in the papers as the "Cannibal Cop?" With women reaching out to me, fully knowing all of the circumstances surrounding my situation and wanting to talk, meet, and have me tie them up, it has given me a glimmer of hope that I can date and experience companionship with a woman again.

"Jails and prisons are filled with pissed off and easily excited people and I was no exception."

Uncle Fester

UNCLE FESTER is a legend in underground publishing. He is the author of books on how to make meth, bombs, and all sorts of interesting things. One of his books helped a cult in Japan make nerve gas that they used to murder scores of people. He wrote his first book while in prison. He did this interview over a series of months, writing me an answer to a question here and there, before he went to work in the morning. You can find his work on his website, where he calls himself "The Most Dangerous Man in America."

You were in prison when you wrote *Secrets of Methamphetamine Manufacture*. Can you tell me about the thought process you were going through when you started to write the book?

Jails and prisons are filled with pissed off and easily excited people and I was no exception. I was particularly pissed off at the narrow-minded people who objected to my study of the sciences. Everybody I know liked and enjoyed my products, so why the big commotion? The trigger which set me at writing the first edition of *Secrets of Methamphetamine Manufacture* was watching Barbara Walters on an evening TV news show railing against "terrorist publishers" and their horrible books about explosives and other areas of forbidden knowledge. That was when it dawned on me that I had plenty of free time and could put it to productive use sharing my areas of forbidden knowledge. I've always had a talent for writing and storytelling, so the field was a perfect fit for me. I simply had a guy down the cellblock pass his typewriter to me and I went to work on it. Lots of guys in the slam will do legal work in their cells relating to their cases, so I just blended in with them. If only they knew what I was banging out on that typewriter...

You have written a number of books over the years. Other than *Secrets of Meth...*, which ones give you most pride? Are there any that you wish you did not do?

My favorite book besides the *Secrets of Meth...* is *Home Workshop Explosives*.

It is a fun read and it brings back great memories of my days playing with explosives. The laws have become such a joy killer in this area. If you are cooking up and having fun with explosives, the presumption from the heat is that you are some kind of terrorist bent upon mass destruction, and that is what they will charge you with! They have no appreciation of the thrill of watching things go BOOM!

The one book I regret doing is the *Bloody Brazilian Knife Fightin'* book. I don't know anything about the subject and I was involved in the project as a translator. It has also been a commercial failure. It goes to show that one should not step outside their genre.

The Aum Cult in Japan used your book *Silent Death* as their tech manual to create nerve gas, which they then used to kill people. What other ways have your books been used that people might not be aware of?

The answer to this one involves my *Secrets of Meth…* book, and it may surprise you. Back when I was cooking, and after that through the first decade or so of my writing career, the primary source of meth production was individual experimenters, biker gangs and a few mobsters. Some of these might be considered to be shady people, but they are my people and domestic. It is for them that I produced the many editions of *Secrets…* to keep them a step or two ahead of law enforcement.

Then beginning in the mid to late 1990s foreign cartels and gangs began to realize the huge amount of money that could be made by producing and smuggling meth. It started with Mexican gangs in the 1990s who would smuggle the starting ingredients from Mexico, set up shop in a desert shack location and turn out a few hundred pounds in a matter of a few days before abandoning said location. They were using the HI and red P reduction process of ephedrine or pseudoephedrine that is ideal for quick mass production using very simple equipment. Then as ephedrine or pseudoephedrine became more difficult to obtain even in Mexico, they switched to the processes and supply tactics using phenyl acetone detailed in my book. These are more involved processes and require a fixed location to set up a proper shop, but that's not a problem south of the border if they pay off the right people. The country is thoroughly corrupt.

Mexico is not the only place this has occurred. The same thing has happened in the Far East, and Australia is their prime export market. Similarly, the mid-east has become a hotspot for large-scale production, with Europe as their export location. Cooking in the mid-east has become easy with all the chaos going on there. All of these locations share the one source of supply for their starting materials: China. They produce materials you would never think would be available on huge scales and as a kicker promise to help get them through customs. If it's not specifically illegal there, they openly run shop and make huge cash delivering precursors.

It used to be that if you could cook some good meth, you were a rock star. Now the stuff is all over the place and just a commodity. Who wants to take the effort to learn the *Secrets of Meth...* if it can be had on any given street corner? This whole situation has become very disappointing to me.

To many people there is this whole moral and cultural code that some things are okay to talk about, and write about, while other things are not. If you write a how-to book about how to be a better parent you are good, if you write a book about how to make LSD, you are bad. Do you ever feel any sense of self-doubt around your work?

I teach the sciences and I entertain with good literature while doing it. Yes. The topics I cover are off the beaten path, but that is part of their allure. Forbidden knowledge is the best kind! I'm a deconstructionist and I do social engineering by means of paperback books. While I entertain people with forbidden knowledge, I also expose them to trains of thought that they probably have never encountered. I try to instill in their thinking that we don't have to accept things as they are and that resistance is not futile. For most people, that's as far as it goes. For those who go farther and try cooking a batch or two, I just hope that they be careful and stay out of trouble.

You used to be with the ridiculously awesome publisher Loompanics, which is sadly no longer in existence. How are you finding the world of publishing now? Which of your books sell the best? Anything new on the horizon?

The world of publishing certainly has changed and not for the better. It seems that books are going the way of the dinosaurs and everybody wants downloads. They expect to get them for free too! This is terribly disheartening for me. The pirated downloaded material is much more easily hidden on a jump drive than a book. Law enforcement would always wave around copies of my books in court as a way of showing intent, so I can understand that angle.

My next project could take one of two directions. I could collaborate with a couple of people in Canada who have perfected the process of making ephedrine using yeast and produce a smaller book with them. It turns out that wine yeast is very good at doing this conversion to ephedrine so long as the brew mixture is allowed access to air while brewing. This would be narrow in scope, but very useful to people who have been frustrated by the 'show ID' laws for pseudoephedrine and ephedrine.

The other possibility would have to wait until I am semi-retired in a few years so that I would have the time and energy to do it. That possibility would be the ninth edition of *Secrets of Meth*... Whichever one I do next, they will be printed on newsprint to make scanning the pages for pirate upload much more difficult. I might even print it in a funny shade of purple to make scanning even more difficult. *Atlas Shrugged* was all about what happens when people's work is stolen from them. The answer is that they won't work to produce more to be stolen.

My bestseller has always been the *Secrets of Methamphetamine Manufacturing* book, and it is by far the most widely downloaded work. My explosives book and my poisons and chemical warfare book were both at one time pretty popular. They are both great reads on interesting subjects. A state of paranoia has set in with people being afraid of being identified as potential terrorists. Innocent knowledge seekers are afraid to touch them.

Robin Raged

ROBIN RAGED is a freelance writer who was once homeless, was once a convict, and is now a self-described activist. He was kind enough to share his experiences from when he lived in a community of homeless folk in the woods of my hometown of Portland, Maine. He mentions a place called Amistad in this story. I used to work there; they fired me for using my personal email to register for fetish sites. Fuck them, right? The area in which Robin lived just a few years ago, has been cleared so that luxury condos can be built. Robin is now employed, and he and his dog are no longer homeless.

Can you tell me a bit about how you got to a place in your life when you wound up camping?

Alcohol. If everything and all of it were boiled down into one factor that lead me to the streets and then to the woods it would be alcoholism.

I was raised in an upper-prole, conservative republican family with every reason to succeed. I had a good upbringing, good schools, good connections, but, I also had something within me that the adoption papers would have no place to put a check next to—I had the "gene"—alcoholism, beneath a couple of other winners: anxiety and depression. The latter pair triggered the former rather late in life for an alcoholic—I was nineteen—but from there it followed the same predictable pattern that every alcoholic/problem drinker staggers through. By the time I was in my mid-forties, I'd been to numerous jails, detoxes, outpatient programs and two trips to prison. When I left prison for the second time, in 2011, there was nothing left to go back to. My parents were gone. The house I'd always assumed would one day be mine was gone. My family, having suffered through enough of my antics was gone as well.

When I left prison, back in 2011, I'd assumed that I'd be heading back to Augusta, from where I'd come, but with much pressure and pleading from prison officials and probation officers, I ended up at one of those dysfunctional Shalom House shelters in Portland. Dysfunctional because this was no "dry" shelter. As long as the rent got paid, the booze and the pills flowed in and

"...if you stay where you're supposed to, we'll leave you alone. Much like a reservation for the less fortunate, a place where the rest of society doesn't have to see them."

out and soon enough I was quite drunk again. Within months I'd left Shalom, had moved in with a fellow, former inmate. This lasted two months and what followed were short stays with friends and longer stays at the Motel Six (where all good stories begin).

I was luckier than many of the newly homeless and when there was no money left and I became truly newly homeless, I was taken in for the winter by an elderly Iraqi Kurdish gentleman and then by a drug addicted former fisherman and finally by another Iraqi—this one non-Kurdish. When this last fellow was arrested I was truly on the street. I had a donated tent and sleeping bag, some donated clothing and a small dog (purchased while drunk at the Motel Six).

But let me backtrack for a moment, pick up a piece of important information I left behind a paragraph or so ago.

During my last few weeks at the Motel Six, with my dog, plenty of booze and a woman of ill repute, I also had a therapist out of Homeless Health in Portland. With her help, we arranged for me to attend an intensive outpatient program. The way that my drinking was going, I was going to die within the year, I was sure. My doctor decided to put me on something new, the combination of Naltrexone (yes, Narcan) and Gabapentin for treating my alcoholism. My physician had read a paper that showed that the combo held great promise in treating alcoholism. I'd like to get into more detail here, but I won't. I'll just say that after three months on these medications, my compulsion to drink was gone. So, as Bella (my little dog) and I became officially homeless, I was coincidentally, luckily, clean and sober.

What kind of person camps, as opposed to one that stays in a shelter?
I'd been to the shelter a total of three times, and used it for what it was. I'd get there late, get out at wake-up and that was that. By the time I became homeless I'd felt as though I'd lost my citizenship sixteen or seventeen times already. I was tired of having "keepers" whether they be prison guards, shelter staff, probation officers, sponsors, even the kind people willing to let me sack on their floors.

When I hit the woods, there was none of that. None at all. Surely we were outlays, trespassing constantly and consciously on forbidden railroad territory, but even in this illegal existence was more freedom than I or the dog had known in years. Despite the threat of police, city and railroad and drunken, rogued-out parsers, we felt free.

Truly. It was a feeling that every person should feel, that supertramp feeling of "free" that can only be truly appreciated when following a period of not free. We pitched our tent (I'd only been camping twice) filled it with our possessions, our blankets.

Others came, and why the woods, why not the shelter? We had teenaged couples that weren't allowed to couple at the teen center, we had those banned from the shelters due to drugs or threats of violence. We had political activists down there experiencing the life and we had a couple of hardcore campers who never intended to live in square society again. ("The city is full of squares and corners. Even your bed, your chair, the rooms, the roads," the Ragman would testify.)

I thought that everyone should live in the woods and really, I wish that we all could.

What was your average day like when you were camping?
The best time to be up was by six at least. By seven all of our tents and gear would be broken down and stashed, all before the railroad cop might show up, usually around eight. A motley, dark skinned crew we were (those of us who left; some stayed) by 7:30AM we were at Amistad, just up the street where each morning a gentleman in a red pickup would hand out cheap pastries and cheap cigars. Some stayed at Amistad, the rest of us moved on, up State Street and then down Congress, acquiring a newspaper or two along the way. Following breakfast at the soup kitchen, the addicts went their ways, to the clinic or onto some other hustle. The rest of us would take out battered instruments down to the old port, busking for enough money to buy friendlier drugs such as spice or weed. Then lunch at the soup kitchen, more of the previous, and then dinner at the soup kitchen. It was usually safe to return to the woods by 7PM if you wanted to skip dinner. At light, the eight the final core would have made their way back to the woods and we'd reassemble in a place we called "Haymarket Square" for music, pilfered food and conversation. Tents up. Lights out.

Why didn't everyone go to the woods? It was illegal. It was too outside of the box for many and I just don't mean legally. Staying at the shelter showed an inherent trust in the system, trust that this was supposed to be and that if one just kept coloring between the lines everything would work out okay. This isn't so for everyone, as the alarming rate of overdoses in the last few years have proven.

You were safer in the woods. But that's not how they would have it be.

Back when I was growing up, there was an area down near St John Street where people camped. All of that area is gone. Is this progress? Condos replacing camps?
Twenty years ago and the hobo camps were pretty much left alone. Officer Dan Knight told me that twenty years ago they'd actually drop drunks off in the woods, knowing that they'd be cared for by the other residents. Today it's different and it's not so much the legality or illegality as it is development and

containment. Much like the Native Americans that went before them, the policy today concerning the homeless is to keep them where you can see them. Or, rather, not just where anyone can see them, but where the proper authorities can see them, while the moneyed tourist does not. Of late the message to the homeless population has been: if you stay where you're supposed to, we'll leave you alone. Much like a reservation for the less fortunate, a place where the rest of society doesn't have to see them.

They're still there.

I could spend a bit of space here on development, but I'll leave it to this: I was actually grateful for the railroads for a time. They kept the property they confiscated from being developed.

You are housed now. Do you miss it? Any of it? All of it?
I'm in a house now, and I'm certainly grateful. As much as I like to glorify the outdoors, it's a bit like living the life of a pilgrim, and the weather sucks. Still, I miss the camaraderie. I miss being in good physical shape without trying. I miss being no one's bitch. And no matter how you do the math, if you live in society and aren't a member of the clan Koch, you're gonna be someone's bitch.

Well, maybe I just haven't been out of the woods long enough.

"I would class myself as a Satanic Luciferian, aspiring for a more Jehovian stance on life."

Mike Scott

A church that, in theory, worships Jesus and Satan equally, was tied to Charles Manson, and has a symbol that looks more than a tad like a swastika, is bound to get a little attention. While these days no one gives a toss about the Process Church of Final Judgment and its founder Robert DeGrimston, back in the day they freaked people out on a regular basis. They still exist. I spoke to MIKE SCOTT, the lead singer of punk band Lay it on the Line, and also a member of the Process Church of Final Judgment, about what is happening with the Final Judgment today.

There has always been some sort of mystery around the Process Church, how were you drawn to it initially?

I can only go from my history lessons on the subject and listening to those who were there at the time, but the Process Church was built on aloofness and I'm sure it only became more insular as the press continued to misinterpret activities and lawsuits were lost. I'm sure this still attracts people because even in the age of the Internet, where ignorance is more choice than anything, it is not easy to dissect the wheat from the chaff on the subject of The Process Church of the Final Judgment. Most links from Google are superficial sensationalism—with the majority talking about The Church as a dead entity, which perished in the 1970s. I guess for me, the attraction started off as mere curiosity, before I came across people who still talked highly of the teachings. You will find imagery and the like of The Church very quickly with Google searches. The imagery has spread to certain corners of music culture. When this takes your imagination away, then you may possibly, like I did, locate the original speeches and writings of Robert DeGrimston and attempt to use them as others have for, what is closing in on, half a century.

Worshiping both Jesus and Satan thing tends to confuse people and freak them out. Why do you think people are so close-minded about that kind of thing?

Just to clarify—I actually doubt there are any Processeans who worship Christ and/or Satan. The majority (I would hazard a guess anyway, based on personal conversations) are agnostic or atheist. The Great Gods represent more the typical polars of human feeling and action. Satanic Processeans don't worship Satan; rather they follow what would be deemed as a lifestyle based on an almost nihilistic belief in acting as you wish to indulge your baser instincts. I would class myself as a Satanic Luciferian, aspiring for a more Jehovian stance on life. This all has little to do with a belief in those gods as they are in the Bible. The Process could have been created on an Islamic or Hindu mainframe if DeGrimston had put his mind to it, I'm sure.

People love drama and sensationalism. One of the last taboos I suppose is Satanism. Which is ridiculous really. It just helps label the Process Church as 'the other'—the opposite of traditional Christianity. The antithesis. In reality, it is nothing of the sort. In the Internet age, anyone who wants to find that out for themselves will do. Everyone else will choose to believe things how they wish them to be. So be it.

The Church was founded by Robert DeGrimston. What sort of influence has DeGrimston had on you personally?
Personally, I find his writing to be just inspirational. They can read dated at times (first reading of texts for me, for example, were tainted by most references in masculine rather than neutral form—'a man does x; he does y'— it doesn't sit well with me) but the arguments and the logic are timeless. The man was (and/or is) clearly a genius of philosophy and psychology. Timothy Wyllie says as much in his published book about his time in The Church. DeGrimston's efforts to rationalize existence and the futility of existence are simply life changing. His works for me have been an aid to mindfulness as much as anything else I've ever studied. I myself identify as an agnostic who is troubled by humanity's arrogance in assuming we can 'know' God, or 'know' there is no higher power outside of our understanding. The Church and Robert's teachings (for me at least) take a similar initial stance to my gut reaction. They give my life a position and meaning that I was lacking previously.

What kind of membership do you guys have right now? Do you want The Church to grow? Do you care?
My opinions will differ hugely from other Processeans, I'm sure. But due to relative scarcity of Processeans, we are united not by geographical Chapters as The Church was back in the day, but by the Internet and increased access to teachings. My efforts have been to try to offer those who want to know more the chance to do so. I, and I would guess any other Processean too, have no interest in promoting The Process further than that. By definition, The Church is

not self-advertising. That is a purpose that defeats the object of The Process. I would have appreciated an easier task in uncovering the teachings in the first place though, so that is something, as I said, I do like to help with.

What is next for the Process Church?
Nothing vastly different, I'm sure. It is a personal voyage that takes a lifetime. It will not die, nor will it gain huge precedence. So be it.

"I love drugs a lot. I use marijuana, alcohol, cocaine, heroin, and benzos. You want a list?"

Shilo Murphy

SHILO MURPHY is the Executive Director of the People's Harm
Reduction Alliance, and is one of the founders of the Drug Users
Union. He loves drugs. He told me so on the phone. I have no reason
to doubt him. Shilo has gone from being homeless to being the
leader of one of the most influential peer run needle exchanges
in the country. They provide clean meth and crack pipes, needles
for heroin, and are strong advocates for drug users nationwide.

Can you tell me a bit about what you guys do at the People's Harm Reduction Alliance?

Sure, we are a needle exchange, we are non-profit, and we get no government money. We operate in five counties over two different states. We do mobile delivery by either car or bicycle and of course we have a physical site. We are run by drug users, our board of directors, staff and volunteers has to be 51% active drug users. We put the people we serve in charge of making decisions. I see so many places that are dealing with drug users that have no active drug users on their board and their staff, which makes no sense to me. The PHRA [People's Harm Reduction Alliance] has been in existence for twenty-five years, I have been working here for twenty and have been head of the alliance for eight years. Our philosophy is simple. We love you just the way you are. We want you to be the best damn drug users you can be. I love drugs a lot. I use marijuana, alcohol, cocaine, heroin, and benzos. You want a list?

I have read quotes from you when you talk about the difference between chaotic drug users and stable drug users. So with you loving drugs a lot, and other people loving drugs a lot, how do you define chaotic versus stable when it comes to drug use?

You are aware if you are chaotic. Drugs are negatively affecting you and your life. You are always in chaos, you're always stressed out. Our goal is to get people into stable drug use, even if they want to stop using drugs we can help with that too. Basically, everyone in the country uses drugs; if you use coffee you're using drugs, if you drink alcohol you use drugs, or if you eat a fucking chocolate bar you're hooked on sugar. So we just decided to make certain drugs illegal, and demonized the people that use them, and certain drugs socially acceptable. It is like our country has declared war on a certain segment of people.

Do other people in the harm reduction movement give you a hard time about how you do things?
Yeah they do. The harm reduction community has always had a problem with drug users in a position of power. I think harm reduction is a philosophy, not necessarily something one does to help during a human rights struggle. We are a human rights organization that happens to do disease prevention and that also happens to do harm reduction. We support harm reduction in philosophy and in fact I wish that more organizations would actually do harm reduction instead of just saying they are doing it. Our goal is to make sure we as drug users, make sure that our brothers and sisters are taken care of, are not dying and are in places of love and respect.

On a panel at a harm reduction conference in Austin you said "Heroin saved your life." You were criticized for that. One leader in the harm reduction movement said that by saying that, you set the movement back twenty-five years. What do you do when people criticize what you do? Do you get a lot of kickback like that?
Drugs did save my life and change my life in a positive way. Years ago we stopped letting people who criticize us dictate how and what we do. We pretty much just stopped responding to people, and when we stopped doing that, most people stopped complaining. We are going to do what we are going to do, whether people complain or not. If someone puts up something on the Internet about how much we suck, we post it on our Facebook page. It's always going to be about a conversation with a lot of people, and we know that.

How can someone be the best drug user they can be?
There are all sorts of ways that can happen. They can support each other and love each other and have all of their life's desires fulfilled as a drug user. You can have the life you want, you can have relationships, have good jobs, make money, have friends, you can really have anything you want in life and still be a drug user. We just want you to be the best drug user you can be and we will help you do that. People kept coming to our program and saying they wanted needles to do meth with because they didn't have access to a pipe, so we give out crack pipes, and meth pipes. We give out Naloxone, not just to people that are using, but to their family members and friends too. We can try to hook you up with the Drug Users Union that I co-founded.

The Drug Users Union, also called the Urban Survivors Union, has three chapters in San Francisco, Seattle, and Greensboro North Carolina, Each chapter has somewhere between fifty and one hundred members. The basic premise is that non-drug users are always trying to make positive changes on our behalf, but they always suck at it, they are always trying to save us, but we don't want to be saved. We don't need to be saved. Our goal is to put ourselves in charge of our own lives, both locally and at a national level. Active drug users can come together and organize and better their lives, engaging politicians and trying to end laws that discriminate against drug users.

Our system and our society spend trillions of dollars fighting a drug war that does little or nothing, in changing people's use. We have to try something different. It is time for us to focus on love and respect and kindness—that will do more to change someone than anything else. If you are told you are loved, and told you are worth it, and told you will be here tomorrow and that you can fulfill your lifelong dreams, your life will be more productive than if you are told that you are a bad person.

"...can an institution specifically designed to harm its occupants ever actually be rehabilitative?"

Ben Gunn

BEN GUNN was convicted of a murder that he committed when he was still a teenager, and served thirty-two years in prison. During that time he broke the rules as much as he possibly could. One of the ways he did so was to write a blog from prison that explained just how fucked up things were in there. He is now a free man and through his business Mokurai Consulting, he is a prison survival consultant and a campaigner working on justice and prison issues.

Can you tell me a bit about how you wound up in prison?
I rarely talk about the details of my crime in public. I find it prurient, but I also have to bear in mind that my victim's family may read what I say. In a strange way, murder is both a very public yet very private crime.

Whilst in a children's home, aged fourteen, I had an altercation with another boy. I was holding a piece of wood; he wasn't. I immediately called the police and pleaded guilty at trial.

Although I had no intent to kill my victim, the reality was that I had. Discussions about my relative responsibility are meaningless to me. Because of my actions, a human being died. The legal niceties are less important than that immutable reality.

How did you find prison life? In particular, how did you find being a prisoner that routinely questioned authority?
Prison life was, um, challenging! My first trip to solitary was within days of entering prison. Staff had wrecked my cell during a cell search, and my attitude was fuck your mess, you put it back together. The Governor disagreed.

At that young age, my ire was usually directed at the screw at my door—the visible embodiment of the institution. With staff using regulations to harass, I soon learned that a knowledge of the vast literature that comprises what we can call "the prison rules" can be a weapon for prisoners' defense as well as staff attacks.

My subversion—to pick one of many words—only became coherent once I began my education. Having completed my basic education at the start of my sentence, I only truly took an interest in the wider world and serious ideas in my late teens. My first degree weighed heavily towards political theory and so I found myself in an interesting position—sitting in the State's dungeons whilst absorbing ideas of legitimacy, democracy and the ever-nebulous 'freedom.'

Prison is a total institution. There is no sphere of private autonomy or sovereignty. And yet I had to come to some working accommodation with this entity—my rejecting it didn't make the walls vanish! My broad stance was, is this order legitimate and rational? If so, broadly comply. If not, then I'd refuse to comply.

With education and maturity the targets of my ire shifted from the staff at my door to more elevated vistas—policy makers, senior management.

An interesting point is that with prison being a total institution, just about any act can be an act of resistance, no matter how seemingly trivial. All challenges to the prison are viewed in the same way, as illegitimate.

The Prison Service has, rather cleverly, shifted its labeling of 'subversives.' Whilst this was a term widely used and accepted until the 1990s, it gave this veneer of recognition that the challenge to the prison authority was rooted in some coherent worldview. From the 1990s however, with a huge influx of psychologists into prisons, 'subversives' were relabeled in terms of 'personality disorders.' The Prison Service has redefined any and all challenges to authority as being merely the outward actions of a disturbed mind.

What does prison reform mean to you, and what should prison be in a decent society?
I have made the belated realization that 'prison reform' can be viewed through two very different perspectives. For prisoners, reform means efforts to remove or mitigate the needless oppression of prisoners; essentially, prisoners seek some form of justice. However, for policy makers, reform means to change the penal system so that it is more cost effective, and that it reduces reoffending. These are not mutually exclusive aims of reform, and I argue both are needed for a sustained change. To attempt penal reform without addressing the needs of prisoners is futile in the long term.

The foundation of any legitimate penal reform must rest on using prison sparingly. Every Judge should ask, "Is this person causing such social harm that they need to be confined behind concrete and steel?" Prison must be used for a proper purpose, not as a convenient social dustbin. Within prisons, the purpose of the institution should be to provide the conditions for reform. In continuing to degrade prisoners, we fail in any attempt to recapture them into the community fold.

The question for me is, can an institution specifically designed to harm its occupants ever actually be rehabilitative?

Can you tell me a bit about your consulting service? I was particularly interested in the "prison survival" aspect of things.
I had no real idea of what I would do on release, what barriers or opportunities would exist so that I could continue my broad work of reform. It seemed sensible to form myself into a consultancy, which would provide an umbrella for all my various activities.

One service is Prison Survival. This is an established service in the US, with some potential prisoners being guided through the experience by experts (often ex-cons). As I expected, this part of my consultancy has not grown. As I have seen in other jurisdictions, British defendants tend to be less professional in their approach!

My activities are eclectic, ranging from media work, public speaking, to advising policy makers in both the public and private sector.

How is life today? Who are you now?
Nearly four years after my release, I have yet to find my place in the world. The structures and society in prison offered avenues for me to imbibe a meaningless existence into something with meaning. I was the politician, the rabble-rouser, and the jailhouse lawyer. My status within prison society was known and meaningful (if only to me).

The wider world holds so many possibilities, I'm not sure if I any longer care for such labels or social position. Each day, I have to find meaning in my new life. I sit in Office of Power, and I sit in the gutter. Strange life.

For over a year now, I have suffered debilitating bouts of depression and anxiety—an awful combination! To expect thirty-two years of imprisonment to leave me unscathed was rather optimistic, and I am using this period of quietude as one of reflection.

"It was a double-edged sword; they dug to discredit me but also found many of the things I said to be accurate and true."

Jesse Macbeth

To some JESSE MACBETH is a war protestor; to others he is a ridiculously bad person who falsely claimed that he was an Iraq War Veteran. He didn't just claim he was a veteran though, he said all sorts of things to the media about his fellow soldiers murdering and raping civilians that he claimed he witnessed when he was a soldier. He was convicted of making false statements to the U.S. Department of Veteran Affairs and sentenced to five months in prison. He is the founder of the Alkebulan Community, which is a group of African centered families working and living in Georgia. Their goal is to separate from a society and system they feel is oppressive, and built on pitting people against each other.

I read something you wrote once that said that you had joined the military, but were harassed and humiliated because you were a Muslim, is that true?

Yes, this is true. I was beat near to death, stripped of my clothes and tied to the pole of the trying bay for three days. During those three days I was beat some more, had pages of my Quran ripped out and shoved down my throat, had bacon shoved down my throat, was pissed on, and was subject to tons of racial and ethnic slurs. My medical records at Martin Army community hospital at Fort Benning, GA, can confirm my injuries.

Was that part of the thought process around telling the media things that were not true about your military experience?

When you have spent months trying to talk to lawyers and police, trying to get justice for the torture and humiliation I went through at the hands of the U.S. Army, just to be told that they won't take the case because they don't want to go up against the Army, it takes you to a point where you have a couple of options. You grab a weapon and go on to the nearest base and start shooting or you plan and calculate your moves. You spend time researching groups that would gladly tell your story because it feeds into their already biased agenda.

You know what you say and do will cause a backlash. The beautiful thing about social media and getting stuff out there is that someone will believe, no matter what it is. Me being a Muslim who speaks Arabic, and grew up in that culture, knows the trigger words and what to say. The best revenge I could have gotten was exactly what I did. I made the army look like the bigoted terrorists they are and let Arabs know these are the horrible things American soldiers are told to do. Thus inciting anti-American sentiments and causing the deaths of more U.S. terrorists. That was my goal back then. I got my revenge and now I feel sated.

You said that soldiers raped and tortured civilians, even though you did not see those things with your own eyes. Do you think they really happened? Or is what you said a lie?
I know those things really happened. The media reports in both English and Arabic confirm these things went on and continue to go on. The only part of that that was a lie is that I did not witness it or partake in it, for I was never deployed and even if I was deployed I would never do these types of things anyway. I am first and foremost a soldier of Allah. Islam will always come first in my life. If I was actually deployed out there and I saw this crap going on I would have slaughtered any and every American soldier that was doing it. Of course, America would vilify me for it while condoning the torture and terrorizing of innocent Muslims. I would probably be dead, but as you know, we as Muslims don't fear death, we only fear Allah. I actually credit myself for helping to expose these atrocities and bringing them to light. If you look at the timeline of when these things came to light it was shortly after I went viral and the world started digging to debunk me. It was a double-edged sword; they dug to discredit me but also found many of the things I said to be accurate and true.

You are now running the Alkebulan Community. Can you tell me a bit about that and what it stands for?
This community has evolved a lot. It started out as purely a black and Muslim community, and effort to get us to own something and separate from a society that hates us. It changed to a Muslim based community that is a staging ground for revolution. Not a violent revolution but a revolution nonetheless. Now we accept anyone and everyone who wants to fight against oppression and a system that was built on oppressing some and elevating others, a system that feeds on and gains power from division, pits races against each other, men against women, religions against each other etc. Amid the chaos the system profits and does what it wants because a people divided is easily conquered. So in Alkebulan community we build and unplug from the system. We don't rely on them for anything, meaning we control our own resources. Our ultimate goal is to take over one city at a time. We do this by playing the systems game. We get

the support of the local communities and start to put our own people into office until we eventually have one of our own in a position of power in that city. So, if we control that city's government, police forces, treasury, become governor and mayor, then we control that city, and all those we put in power answer to the leaders of Alkebulan Community. We effectively control a city without firing a bullet. Once we have control of one city we move on to the next and repeat. Eventually we will have so much influence, presidential candidates will reach out to us and ask what they can do for our voting block. It's their politics. This is how we silently take over.

What do you hope this community will become?
An example of how to destroy an empire.

"You will feel that he is vaguely pathetic, because he's the kind of guy who still has a waterbed, and his Sexbot looks more like a store mannequin than a person."

Patrick Quinlan

PATRICK QUINLAN is the author of a number of books, including the *Los Angeles Times* best selling novel *Smoked*. At one point he was going to run for Governor of Maine but dropped out of the race after announcing his candidacy. He recently wrote a book called *Sexbot*. Because of this he has become a bit of an expert on sex robots, and interviewed on the subject for numerous websites and publications.

Do you think there ever might come a time when sexbots are totally normal? That you go over to your buddy's house to watch the game and have a beer and just see a sex robot sitting in the corner? How far away is that?

Normalcy is an insidious thing. The word insidious sounds bad, but I don't really mean it that way. All I mean is that normalcy has this funny habit of changing ever so gradually, until it's completely different from what it once was, but no one really notices.

Take porn as an obvious example. When I was a twelve-year-old kid, porn was hard to come by. You tended to find porn magazines in garbage dumpsters, or under the bed when you broke into some guy's apartment while he was out at work. Getting your hands on porn was something that happened once in a rare while. The closest thing to a computer anybody had in those days was Atari.

Nowadays, if you're a twelve-year-old kid, porn is on the computer and right at your fingertips. To avoid porn, you would have to be this devoutly religious kid and try not to look at it.

That didn't come about overnight. It happened gradually, and now it's totally normal. There was a time when porn was against the law. Now it's what's for breakfast. Did people shout and scream while the change was happening? Sort of. But a lot less than you would have expected.

By the way, I've had people write to me about my book Sexbot in a complaining tone, and say, "This isn't porn." Yes, I know it isn't. Haven't you seen enough porn by now?

SUBVERSIVE

I guess my point is that things change. What was once strange and exotic becomes normal. And it happens step-by-step, gradually, so it seems like nothing is happening.

I think the first real sexbots will be around in a few years from now, but they will be so expensive that only very rich people can afford them. Slowly they will come down in price, like big flat screen TVs did. Your cousin, the disbarred lawyer, will turn up with one, but it will be sort of a rudimentary model. You will feel that he is vaguely pathetic, because he's the kind of guy who still has a waterbed, and his sexbot looks more like a store mannequin than a person.

Eventually, you will go over to somebody's house and there will be two or three sexbots hanging around in bikinis, chatting and flirting with the guests. The only way you will be able to tell them apart from real young women is that they will be physically perfect, and they will be showing sexual interest in fat middle-aged bastards who you know for a fact are not multimillionaires. This will happen sooner than any of us think, and we will hardly notice it happening until afterwards.

There is a lot of judgment of people that want to bang a robot. Is that what good people do? Look down on people because they want to do sexual shit that is not natural? Or do we all just let our freak flag fly?
Looking down on people who do out-of-the-ordinary things is the glue that holds our world together. It keeps the status quo. Once you allow people to start doing things that were forbidden before, that's when change happens. And that's when the future comes, good or bad.

We are in a time of great change. So much change that barely anyone seems to remember what it was like before. Oh, curmudgeons write in to the comments sections on websites, bemoaning this or that lost social more, but no one cares what they think. At first people will feel weird when other people start having sex with robots. Older people will judge them harshly. "That's not how it was in my time." Younger people will wish they could afford a sexbot.

After a while, it will all seem totally normal. Why not have a sexbot? One day, people won't just want to have sex with robots—they'll want to marry robots. This will be because the robots will have all the good jobs.

There will be robots doing all kinds of things. Global warming wiped out the polar bears? Hey, you can have a big friendly robot polar bear that lives in your home with you—it's even better than a real polar bear because it doesn't want to kill you and eat you. And it talks! Your sexbot can ride your polar bear like a horse! How awesome will that be?

How did you get on to sexbots for something to write about?
I had lunch in the dining car of the New York to Miami Amtrak train. And the neat

thing about the dining car on the train is there are only about ten tables, so they make you sit with people you don't know.

So one day I ate lunch with this rich pervert, a Boston real estate developer, who is afraid of flying. That's why he was on the train. And when I say rich, I mean tens of millions of dollars rich. One tenth of 1% rich.

This guy, who has had trouble with women (and probably people in general) his whole life, told me that soon, there will be lifelike sex robots. I hadn't really spent much time contemplating this idea before.

So this real estate developer told me that sexbots were coming soon— as soon as sex toys like Real Doll could be wed to advanced robotics and artificial intelligence. He thought this would happen in five to seven years (the conversation took place two years ago), and that the robots would likely cost about $100,000 apiece.

At that price, he said he planned to buy three of them.

You have been quoted as saying "There are men, in particular, that want women who are beautiful, agreeable, forever young, ever eager for sex, and who don't have a lot to say." That pisses some women off a tad. How prevalent do you think this school of thought is in a man?
I think that significant minorities of men feel this way. I don't know why a comment like that would piss anyone off, unless it was someone who doesn't like to deal with reality.

Notice what a lot of wealthy men do as they grow older. They wind up with increasingly younger women. Beautiful women, in many cases, who are decades younger than they are. Why would this be true? Because of the scintillating conversation? Probably not. Being an old and rich man, and having a beautiful young woman with you, is a lot like having a sexbot. And generally speaking, rich people do things that a lot of not-rich people would do if they had the money. Everybody is shallow, women and men. We're hard-wired that way. It's part of how we've managed to populate every corner of this poor, overburdened planet.

Robots bring to mind immortality. Why do you think someone would want to stay alive forever? Do you want to die?
The short answer is no, I don't want to die. And I think it's clear why someone would want to live forever—mostly because we don't know what happens after we die, and it seems possible that we cease to exist. I don't know about you, but I don't want to cease to exist. Which brings me to a slightly longer answer. You saw that Darryl Dawkins recently died, right? You probably remember him from when he was a pro basketball player—I sure do. He used to dunk the ball so hard that he shattered the glass backboard a couple of times. They had

to change the way they manufactured the baskets because of him. When he was a player, he was so vital, so energetic, and so alive—both physically and personality-wise—that it seemed unlikely he could ever die. It actually seems more likely that he never existed in the first place. He was a daydream we all imagined. If Darryl Dawkins never existed, that suggests we don't exist either, at least not in the way we appear to. It's a liberating thought.

Which brings me to one last idea. In my book Sexbot, people can achieve a sort of immortality by downloading their human awareness into intelligent machines. Suppose for a minute that this were possible. You are no longer your body—in fact you are divorced from it, liberated from it. Since you are inside a machine, now you are essentially a computer program.

Not only could you live a long time, possibly forever, you could live in any way you choose. You wouldn't have to look like a person. You could be a submarine at the bottom of the ocean, or a star cruiser traveling into deep space. You could be a sexbot, if you wanted, or some kind of weird warrior RoboCop. If you're the brainy type, you could choose to be a bot crawling the interwebs, digesting information.

Weirder still, you could be one of these things for a time, and then choose to be something else entirely. Or you could copy and paste yourself, and be all of these things at once.

That's the immortality I dream of for you and me.

Mike Maharry

MIKE MAHARRY is the Communications Director at the Tenth Amendment Center. It says on their website "Less Democrat, less Republican, more constitution," and that pretty much sums it up. They describe themselves as the nation's leading source for constitutional education and nullification activism. Mike, and the organization he represents, wants more power at the state level, and he wants the feds to get off of his lawn.

Can you tell me a little bit about what the Tenth Amendment Center is all about?

You can sum up the philosophy of the Tenth Amendment Center (TAC) in a simple sentence: follow the Constitution every issue, every time, no exceptions, no excuses. Our work rests on the founding era understanding that the Constitution created a union of states that maintain their political sovereignty except within those areas they delegated power to the general government. The intended structure of the American system was for the federal government to exercise only limited, enumerated powers. All authority not delegated to the general government remains with the states and the people. James Madison summarized this structure in Federalist #45.

The powers delegated by the proposed Constitution to the federal government are few and defined. Those which are to remain in the state governments are numerous and indefinite. The former will be exercised principally on external objects, as war, peace, negotiation and foreign commerce; with which the last the power of taxation will for the most part be connected. The powers reserved to the several states will extend to all objects which, in the ordinary course of affairs, concern the lives, liberties and properties of the people, and the internal order, improvement and prosperity of the State.

So, most power was to remain at the state level. Regulating health care, religious issues, education, manufacturing, agriculture, safety and really most everything is properly a function of state government. The federal government legitimately has very little authority. But over the history of the United States,

"The U.S. federal government regulates how much water I can have in my toilet. I think that gives you an indication of just how much freedom Americans have."

the federal government has taken more and more power upon itself, leaving the states to function as little more than administrative districts.

Our work at the TAC revolves around education and activism. We teach about the original constitution and the proper role of the federal government, and we advance activism at the state level to rein in unconstitutional federal actions.

Our activism focuses on what is known as nullification. Most simply defined, this is any action or set of actions taken by a state, or even individuals, that serve to render a federal action null, void or simply unenforceable within a state. Thomas Jefferson and James Madison first formalized the principles of nullification in the Kentucky and Virginia Resolutions of 1798, a response to the unconstitutional Alien and Sedition Acts. In a nutshell, Jefferson said nullification was "the rightful remedy" when the federal government oversteps its bounds. Madison put it a different way, say a state was in duty bound to "interpose" to arrest the progress of evil.

The primary action that states can take to nullify a federal act is through simply non-compliance. Madison gave us this blueprint in Federalist #46, writing that "a refusal to cooperate with officers of the Union," would create impediments and obstructions to federal actions.

In practice, the federal government depends on state action, personnel and resources to do virtually everything it does, from enforcing drug prohibition to implementing national health care. When states withdraw that support, the feds lack the resources to enforce their laws or implement their programs themselves. That renders them effectively null and void. The law may remain on the books, but it is unenforced.

Stare legalization of marijuana is probably the best example of this strategy. As more and more states have legalized it either for medical use, or for general use, the feds have lost the ability to enforce federal prohibition.

My personal involvement in the TAC flows out of an even more basic philosophy—any government power is dangerous and subject to abuse. Therefore, if we are going to have government, it should be as decentralized as possible and exercised at the most local level feasible. In the U.S., we now have what I call governopoly. We have monopolized all political authority in Washington, D.C. The system established by the founders was certainly imperfect, but its decentralized nature established some checks and balances. It's not unlike an economic system. The more actors you have in a market, the more competition there is. More choices are available for the consumer. I don't understand why people intuitively understand monopoly is undesirable in the marketplace and they embrace it in government.

Murray Rothbard summed up my views nicely. "In the U.S., it becomes important, in moving toward such radical decentralization, for libertarians and classical liberals—indeed, for many other minority or dissident groups—to begin to lay the greatest stress on the forgotten Tenth Amendment and to try to decompose the role and power of the centralizing Supreme Court. Rather than trying to get people of one's own ideological persuasion on the Supreme Court, its power should be rolled back and minimized as far as possible, and its power decomposed into state, or even local, judicial bodies."

Nullification provides a viable tool to return to a more decentralized system.

What sort of following do you have at this point?
The TAC's influence is growing rapidly as more and more Americans become frustrated with the top-down approach to government in Washington, D.C. Last year, there were over 400 nullification bills introduced in state legislatures across the U.S. addressing issues from gun control to health care to privacy to the drug war.

Would you say you are anti-government? If so, why is that such a scary thing to many people?
It all depends on how you define "anti-government." If you take what the TAC does at face value, it is most certainly NOT anti-government. We are merely advocating for government as it was originally established in the United States. I mean, to say advocate for the Constitution—which is at its very core a document establishing government—is anti-government is nonsensical. But I think a lot of people do view us as anti-government because we emphatically think the federal government should not be doing the vast majority of the things it does. They see us as anti-government because we advocating resisting federal authority. That is viewed as radical and even subversive. But ironically, most of our work involves harnessing the power of the state government—so again, to call that anti-government is nonsensical. Generally, Americans are not comfortable with challenging authority—even illegitimate authority. I suppose it is conditioned into us by public schooling and patriotism. I think that gets channeled into this mindset that any mildly radical departure from the status quo is radical and dangerous. It's anti-government and that makes people nervous.

Ultimately, I don't really care what people call me. I look at it this way— if opposing an institution that wages war around the world, spies on me, regulates what I can put into my body and confiscates upwards of 40% of the fruits of my labor is "anti-government," so be it. I'm not going to apologize for being against that stuff.

I am not saying I agree, or disagree with your viewpoints, but I have always found the thought that Americans are "free" as laughable. Do you have any thoughts on our level of personal freedom in this country?

The U.S. federal government regulates how much water I can have in my toilet. I think that gives you an indication of just how much freedom Americans have.

In all fairness, on some levels, we are relatively free. I mean, I go to church every Sunday and I don't worry about anybody barging in and dragging me off to reeducation camp. I can criticize my government without much concern. In some ways, Americans have more personal freedom than many people in the world. But the toilet water thing is not a joke. The feds mandate that I buy health insurance that conforms to their specifications. Police will lock me in a cage if I decide to grow and ingest certain plants. Cops raid farms for selling raw milk. I have to jump through a million hoops and pay all kinds of fees if I want to start a business. On a million different levels, government micromanages my life. So, I am inclined to agree with you. The idea that we have real personal freedom in the US is a joke. But most Americans would disagree with me. That gives you an idea of how far we've dumbed down the idea of personal freedom.

Where do you see this movement and this country headed?
Honestly, I believe economic realities will ultimately collapse the system. Empire simply isn't sustainable. Trillions and trillions in debt isn't sustainable. The American system will be forced to decentralize because Washington D.C. is going to implode. Sadly, I think it will be a painful process. But I don't know when that will happen. My gut is sooner rather than later, but empires do manage to limp along for a long time. So, it may take years.

In the short term, I think the movement to decentralize will continue to grow. There is so much political dissatisfaction in America right now. This is the perfect opportunity to educate people about the value of political decentralization and personal autonomy. We plan to keep pushing that door open and working to educate as many people as we can. I am by nature an optimist, so I think we will continue to make strides. I'll keep doing all I can regardless.

"I knew I didn't have to
adhere to the guidelines
of Church and State
to determine my own
intellectual, spiritual and
political growth."

Rod Coronado

ROD CORONADO is one of the best known eco-anarchists and animal rights activists of our time. A lot of us sit around talking about how much we care for the planet and animals. Rod feels the same, except he did shit about it that got him thrown in prison. He is out now and working to protect animals in a more lawful way, but one that is hopefully no less effective. He is currently the leader of Wolf Patrol, which describes itself as a conservation movement founded on principles of biocentricity and indigenous cultural preservation.

Without getting into any serious specifics, could you talk a little of your background in activism?

I am descended from the Yoeme indigenous nation, or Yaqui to the outside world. My people come from and live in what today is known as the northern Mexican state of Sonora and southern Arizona. My people have fought the onslaught of western civilization since 1533, and my life and my work is simply the continuation of that. Since the early 1980s I have dedicated my life towards the preservation of all that is still wild and free, most specifically, our animal relations. But I wasn't raised in my homelands or on a reservation, I grew up as a pretty normal middle-class kid, though my parents struggled to provide me with more opportunities than they had. They started out life as farmers in California's San Joaquin Valley, where many Yaquis fled persecution in Mexico to start a new life in America, where soldiers weren't killing us like they were in Mexico. So I gave up the privilege that my parents worked hard to gain, so that I could pursue the passion of not only myself, but my ancestors. I choose to fight the destruction of the natural world, because though Indians aren't being mowed down in America like they once were, our animal relations are, and continue to suffer the consequences of war. For me, such a path isn't a choice, it's an obligation. It's the decision to honor the sacrifices of our ancestors and recognize, that for many, 9/11 is every day and when such terror is being committed, we have an obligation to fight it.

You have done some pretty wild things in the past for your causes. Many people, no matter what their cause, like to talk about what they believe in, but are unwilling to put their freedom on the line for it. Where were you mentally and emotionally to be willing to put it all out there like that?

Although my own struggle has focused on the natural and wild world, having knowledge of the traditions of resistance among indigenous peoples has always been a component of my mental and emotional state. Some people believe in God and Jesus, and have their own divinations, but that God never appealed to me. That God was a malevolent God that represented to the people living peacefully already here, the invasion of their homeland. I believe that the basis of my evolution as a contemporary revolutionary is the knowledge that an alternative worldview existed that mostly only indigenous people still believe in because they know it isn't intellectual concepts, but the way that humans had learned to live harmoniously, with each other and the environment. And guess what? It worked, and existed for thousands of years, without resorting to genocide and war as a means to gain respect.

So once I became aware, I knew I didn't have to adhere to the guidelines of Church and State to determine my own intellectual, spiritual and political growth. I developed mentally and emotionally with role models like Geronimo and Crazy Horse, not white Bible heroes.

How did your experience in prison change you as a person?

Before you can be a warrior, you must recognize that you are choosing a path in which your own safety and security is willingly sacrificed for the sake of others. Tantamount to that is the possibility of physical death and imprisonment, which is the state's greatest deterrent to mass resistance.

So you enter this struggle recognizing that if you get caught, and imprisoned, than you simply join a long line of great people who were imprisoned for their beliefs—Nelson Mandela, Gandhi and many more from every continent. In countries willing to right the wrongs of former rulers like South Africa and Ireland and Nicaragua, political leaders include former revolutionaries who engaged in armed struggle, in manners that today are defined as terrorism. They also were imprisoned for years, and many of them still are. So my own journey through prison was my own personal story of growth and evolution, where I am no longer a free-moving member of society, but a physical prisoner living with hundreds of other men who are similarly removed from society. I used the time to educate myself, keep in good physical and mental health, regularly participated in traditional sweat lodge ceremonies and did my best to help raise awareness within the consciousness of individuals I met in prison, while also learning from these connections too. In prison, we are with the people that capitalism and colonialism created, the people who didn't make good slaves.

So as a revolutionary, you have to recognize that that's an opportunity to help people take back control of their lives and their identity, without using violence, or acts that land you in prison. I've spent a total of six years in prison, but I've always told people I'm not ashamed of what I did to get there. I did what I think a lot of people would have done had they not had the conditioning of society such as that that I rejected. Had they the free will and ability to see when you destroy an ancient forest or treat animals miserably, you are committing a crime much greater than the laws of dominant society.

How does your work with the environment and for the protection of animals relate to colonialism?
My work directly relates to colonialism because I'm fighting the very same attitudes towards nature, animals and people that colonialism embodies and that are still alive today. We're seeing that with wolves in the United States, which have begun to regain a hold in their former territories. This is cause for great celebration, as wolves were one of the most persecuted nations on this continent, similarly bison. So my generation (not just among indigenous thinkers) recognizes now that the genocidal war we waged against wolves, that wiped them out in the early 1900s was a grave ecological mistake, denying the value of these apex predators to their environment or the other people and animals who revered and respected them.

But rather than support wolf recovery, we are seeing politicians and "sportsmen" line up demanding that these vicious predators once again be wiped out, arguing that even natural predation on deer, elk and other natural prey, is a bad thing, because even those wild animals belong to us humans more than wolves. That's the attitude of a colonial, and my people fought it hundreds of years ago, and I continue to fight it today unfortunately.

What is life like for you now? Are you able to work on some causes that you care about?
Since I've completed an eight-year term of federal control, be it pre-sentencing supervision, actual imprisonment and a long term of probationary supervision, I've returned to fight for wolves, bears and other predators in the Great Lakes region where I now live. Every indigenous nation in this area opposes the hunting of wolves, and like me see the similarities between how wolves are viewed and treated, and how indigenous people are still seen today. But in the course of defending wolves, my group, Wolf Patrol has uncovered illegal trapping and baiting, and continue to work to catch poachers. I've found illegal baits, which were treble fish hooks wrapped in meat and meant to be swallowed by wolves and coyotes so that they would die a slow and agonizing death. That's as bad as anything Columbus or Cortez did in my mind. But rather than

be the antagonist, we report such discoveries, and in this one case worked alongside Wisconsin state game wardens to tear them down. These people recognize that I want to help protect "natural resources" like I do, so we work together. That is the kind of revolutionary activity I've been able to continue today. Next month we will be returning to Wisconsin to investigate bear baiting practices. In the one state, over four million gallons of food waste is legally used to lure bear close to hunters at an estimated 60,000 bear bait stations, most of them on public lands. And it's not the bears that are being killed, wolves have been defending their territory and pups against canine invaders which come in the form of bear hunting hounds that are used to pick up the scent of a bear that visited a bait station. Last year nine hunting hounds were killed by a pack in an area of national forest that the state's wildlife agency has delineated as a "wolf caution area." But still bear hunters loosed their dogs in the area, and when they get killed, develop an even greater animosity towards wolves. I haven't been arrested in years, but after just two years in the field, Wolf Patrol's presence has led to local politicians passing a law, "The Right to Hunt Act," which was written specifically with Wolf Patrol in mind. The new law makes it illegal for us to follow hunters or film their activities, despite being on public lands. Governor Scott Walker signed the law at the annual convention of the Wisconsin Bear Hunters Association, symbolizing to me that though my recent actions haven't been illegal, they still are revolutionary enough to cause the destroyers of the wild to once again circle their wagons.

Mason Dwinell

Sungazing is the practice of staring into the Sun for health benefits.
Some sungazers say that one does not need to eat if a sungazer.
This, of course, gives all sorts of people an opportunity to act super
smart, and point out that people actually need food to survive. The
website of MASON DWINELL states that "the sun holds incredible
power for people that wish to obtain it." He was the subject of
the documentary, *Eat the Sun*, and is the author of the book, *The
Earth was Flat: Insight into the Ancient Practice of Sungazing*.

Can you tell me a bit about how you got involved in sungazing in
the first place?
While living in San Francisco at the turn of the century, I was enrolled
at the American College of Chinese Medicine (ACTCM), for four years we
were knee deep in the supernatural, delving into questions: the meaning of life,
immortality, magic, human potential, levitation. Many flavors of the impossible
passed through our radar; stories, gurus, and wanderers shared their curiosities,
spurring us on. A handful of us at ACTCM were searching, digging, practicing.
Toward the end of the program, a lecture was given by HRM (the global sungazing
prophet at the time) on the power of charging the mind through sungazing. The
practice resonated; four of us began getting up early, chasing sunrises.

What benefits do you feel you received from this practice over time?
'Don't look into the sun you'll go blind.' Ha! Our potential is greater than you
could possibly imagine. Sungazing opened the door to so much. Yes, sungazers
have many different experiences. Clean sensations of bliss, comfort, calm,
and peace. Meditation on steroids. However the richest gift may have been
cementing the understanding and knowing that energy is the root of life. We are
all energetic beings. How we metabolize and utilize that energy is for another
discussion. However, having our eyes opened to what is possible is a glorious
and powerful thing. Reigniting the fact that our traditional educational systems
and societal thinking is limiting, short-sighted, and embarrassing.

"With adequate imagination and focus one can manipulate and manifest immaterial into reality"

What about the whole food aspect? Is it true your appetite decreased and you were able to sustain yourself mostly through sungazing?
It is unfortunate the media grabbed hold of the food issue so tightly. I fear that topic takes away from the glory, root, and power of the practice. Yes, my (and some of my peers') appetites decreased. But not all of us, some folks ate more. Sungazing appeared to assist in quenching one's hunger. Clearing the noise and clutter from our system, enabling us to make informed choices, our own choices. As if a light bulb turned on: didn't need to eat, the activity became a choice. For a myriad of reasons besides survival, the option to chow down or not became a choice. As our systems calmed, societal and DNA programming quelled, it felt as though space was created to allow the possibility for clearer decisions. Essentially not blindly reacting to a situation as a lemming, rather gleaning reflection and wonder, all coupled with a mindful realization that we are capable of more, much more.

How much of this is about the powers of the sun, and how much of it is about retraining our mind to do things we did not think were possible?
Perhaps it is a little of both, indeed one concept feeds the other. As with meditation, when you clean out the noise you become aware of the depths of your existence; the possibilities unfold with brilliant potential. All of the necessary information and answers are within us; we simply need to take the time and effort to hear, to feel. With adequate imagination and focus one can manipulate and manifest immaterial into reality.

That said, there is something unique and powerful about sungazing that unquestionably differs from seated meditation. I'm unsure if it is the raw light inspiring photosynthesis as it hits the blood directly passing through the eye. Or, how the light affects the optic nerve, stimulating the thalamus, hypothalamus, pineal gland, pituitary gland, and overall capacity of the brain. In turn bringing more energy, efficiency and light into the entire body. Or maybe it is something else entirely. What I do know, is staring into the sun at sunrise creates experiences and sensations far different from staring into a candle.

Where are you now with this? Do you still practice it? Do you still believe?
Yes, I believe the practice of sungazing can be powerful, wonderful and mind blowing. I have not sungazed in a couple years, alas. I hope to again someday. It takes a fair bit of effort to carve out the time and space to give the practice the respect it deserves.

That said, I feel that the awareness of how we energetically and emotionally engage, react, act, and behave weighs far more in reference to general wellbeing and one's overall evolution. If sungazing helps you get there, amen. If not, well, it's still pretty cool.

"One needs to be very suspicious of anyone who wants to prevent others from seeing what goes on in the world."

Mark Marek

MARK MAREK is the owner of Bestgore.com, a website that offers uncensored videos of often very violent acts. His site posted a video called *1 lunatic 1 Ice Pick*, which features an individual called Luka Magnotta mutilating the corpse of student Lin Jun and more. Because of posting the video Marek was convicted of obscenity charges. He was given a six-month conditional sentence.

How did Bestgore get started? Did you always have an interest in this kind of thing, or did you just see a market for it?

It was a risky undertaking, and I was being discouraged because (1) this isn't the niche that gets top popularity rankings, and (2) when I launched the site—early 2008—the niche was dominated by well-established websites with a firm hold on this corner of the Internet. Still, I entered the seemingly oversaturated market with the goal to deliver what I was missing from other players—background information and descriptive titles.

It came at a cost, as a lot of my time went on doing research and compiling available information about the content. I was putting all this time and effort in, never knowing if anyone will even read my articles. I also made a commitment to myself to never deceive readers, so I always titled my posts descriptively, ensuring a reader knows exactly what they're going to see if they click through. I have never clickbaited anyone with over-exaggerated titles, but also never downplayed the severity of the content within. Turns out, people appreciate this no BS approach, and even though I was a newcomer, readers kept coming back for more and from there it was just up and up.

As for whether I had an interest in this kind of thing, or whether I saw a market for it—I can't say I saw a market. It never even occurred to me there could be a substantial one. I thought people would naturally feel averse to this type of content due to conditioning by the mainstream press, movie industry, education system, etc., and only a few Internet bad assess would actually care. But I definitely had interest in making available to the masses content that was being so nonchalantly censored by other media outlets.

The content published on Best Gore is nothing more and nothing less than a reflection of what really goes on in the world. Pretending that it doesn't go on by not reporting on it will not mean that all that foulness does not take place. I've always been a strong proponent of freedom of the Internet and the free flow of content and ideas on the information superhighway. The other part of the right to freedom of expression is the right to access to information. And so I established Best Gore so the information that is routinely censored by the mainstream press, is available to those who are interested. It is not forced on anyone; so all those who prefer to live with rose colored shades on can just ignore the site. But those who do want to see reality ought to have access to content that exposes it. After all, real-life is uncensored.

How popular is the site?
I used to have Google Analytics on the website, but as part of my commitment to members' privacy, I removed the script in 2012. I didn't feel I could trust Google with information about the readers of Best Gore, and as Edward Snowden's leaks proved a year later, I was right to distrust Google.

I have not collected any user analytics since, and therefore I don't have an idea just how popular the site is, but broadly speaking, there are millions of people reading the website every year.

Until recently, I also used a script that tracked keywords people who landed on the website used in search engines. No identifiable information was collected, just what search term the person searched for when they were referred to the site by a search engine. This exposed just how depraved and sick people who are not Best Gore regulars are. Best Gore regulars access the site directly, either by typing the URL www.bestgore.com into their browser, or by clicking on the bookmark. They don't end up on the site by loading up Google and searching for "eight-year-old pussy destroyed". That's what white knights and social justice warriors do. When they think no one is watching, they search for perverted stuff on the Internet, but when they're done, they won't shut their yaps badmouthing Best Gore, because that's the way to ensure no one suspects them of searching for eight-year-old destroyed pussies on the Internet.

What are the types of things on your site that people tend to be most into?
Content that sparks big discussions and controversy varies. Mexican narco executions, torture and beheadings are traditionally popular because of exceptionally brutal mistreatment of victims, lately there have been several ISIS videos that often matched the brutality, but are also provided in high definition, and generally anything that makes people say: "I thought I've seen it all"—like Luka Magnotta's *1 Lunatic 1 Ice Pick*.

A lot of people think that if something is brutal, sadistic or violent, it

should not be seen, as if by not looking it will just go away. What do you think about that school of thought?

These people are not only dangerous on countless levels, but based on our own metrics, they are the ones behind the vilest acts. After all, virtually every serial killer was a person that was regarded by others as an upstanding citizen, often holding respectable jobs, engaging in community programs, nice to kids, etc. This is why everyone is so surprised when truth about them comes to light, and they're caught saying—*I would never in a million years think he/she could possibly do that*.

One needs to be very suspicious of anyone who wants to prevent others from seeing what goes on in the world. Such people often have an agenda, or have something to hide. Best Gore is in the business of exposing miscreants for who they really are; only people who fear that we'll soon blow their cover and expose them for the miscreants that they are too, would have an interest in shutting Best Gore down. Or they badmouth the site in hopes that it will make them look prude and incapable of bad things, so nobody suspects that when they turn the lights off, they get on the Internet to search for kiddy porn.

People die all the time in truly horrible ways at the hands of our respective governments. It seems that is okay, but watching video of it is not. This is not supposed to be a leading question, but does that make sense to you?

It's ironic that a government would sponsor terrorists, so they could massacre whole towns with weapons and money provided, but would imprison bloggers who expose it. In other words, committing atrocities is OK by our governments, but exposing these same atrocities is a criminal offense. I should know, I've been in prison or on conditional sentences since 2013 for informing the people on the realities of the world. Canadian government will not tolerate the idea of informed citizenry, so myself, as well as dozens of other bloggers, have faced politically motivated prosecution with the goal to silence the dissenting voices. After being held in maximum-security prison (publishing articles on a blog apparently makes me so dangerous, the threat I posed was far too great to jail me with the general population) three times, I was placed under house arrest which I concluded last month, and am currently serving the reminder of my conditional sentence. I was also under full prior restraint for sixteen months, and although I'm no longer bound by prior restraint, I'm on a self-imposed self-censorship due to still being physically held in Canada, where having an opinion that contradicts the majority is punishable by prison. But that's just Canada. No other webmaster who published the content I am being prosecuted for, was prosecuted by their respective country. Canada is the only country in the world with zero tolerance for freedom of expression that does not align with the government's official narrative.

"I had a profound personal multidimensional experience with an apparent interdimensional entity."

Alfred Webre

ALFRED WEBRE is a futurist. He is without a doubt the only man in history to have taught economics at Yale and thinks Jimmy Carter might have been an alien. This is not meant to imply he is wrong. If you check out his work or even read this interview, you will see that Webre brings it for real. He is the author of numerous books. For more information you could check out his website, Exopolitics: Politics, Government, and Law in the Universe.

For those who are not aware, could you tell me a bit about what exopolitics is, and how you became involved in it?

I was raised in an international family in Cuba and the United States, educated at Georgetown Preparatory School in Classics, Yale University, and Yale Law School in International Law, and radicalized by my experience of the Cuban Revolution and my opposition to the Vietnam War. By the end of 1972, I was general counsel to the New York City Environmental Protection Administration, and my two immediate bosses, Mayor John Lindsay and EPA Administrator Jerome Kretchmer, decided to run for U.S. President and Mayor of New York. I felt the conventional 3D-based materialistic paradigm of politics was limiting and had been exploring the multidimensional nature of reality, reading books like Ostrander & Shroeder's *Psychic Discoveries Behind the Iron Curtain*. In January 1973, I decided to leave my formal position in politics and government, became intellectual colleagues with Phillip H. Liss, PhD, a professor of experimental psychology at Rutgers University who was also an expert in parapsychology and extraterrestrial studies. In February 1973 I had a profound personal multidimensional experience with an apparent interdimensional entity. Although I have written a 750-page manuscript around that experience, I still have not concluded whether the entity was a genuine interdimensional intelligent extraterrestrial or spiritual entity, an AI Artificial Intelligence, or a human remote-influencing probe. Nevertheless, that experience served to spur me on in my new fulltime pursuits in the multidimensional world.

By June 1973 I had co-authored my first book in the multidimensional area, The Age of Cataclysm that set out the Context Communication Theory of Extraterrestrial Communications. The Context Communication Theory holds that Extraterrestrial and UFO encounters are symbolic communications from the intelligence behind the encounter to human contactees, much in the same way that a dream is a symbolic communication from one's subconscious mind to one's dreaming or conscious mind. In 1976, Rep. Henry B. Gonzales (D-Tex) invited me to Washington, D.C., to assist him in establishing the House Select Committee on Assassinations (HSCA) to investigate the JFK, RFK, Martin Luther King and Malcolm X political assassinations. Through this work I met members of President-elect Jimmy Carter's inner circle in Washington, D.C., in December 1976. By fall 1977 I had secured the Carter White House agreement for a civilian-led scientific extraterrestrial communication study, of which I was director as a Futurist at Stanford Research Institute.

The CIA and the Department of Defense counter-attacked. In November 1977, the Pentagon liaison to the Stanford Research Institute (SRI) called me into a meeting with administrators and SRI and indicated that if the Carter White House Extraterrestrial Communication Study went forward, the Department of Defense would withdraw all of its studies monies from SRI, then about 25% of its $100 million annual budget. The CIA infiltrated the HSCA and eviscerated its staff findings that these assassinations were in fact political assassinations committed with U.S. government covert resources.

These experiences were my first introduction to practical, on the ground exopolitics by the Draco reptilian, Orion grey, and AI Artificial Intelligence-entrained elements within the U.S. Government, military, intelligence community, and Matrix controllers.

By "Exopolitics" we mean relations among intelligent civilizations in our universe or in any other universe in our multiverse. Thus, for example, Exopolitics is the social science that studied the dynamic interrelations among the Draco reptilian and Orion grey civilizations and others that are under secret Treaty relations with the U.S. government and hence brought about the termination of the proposed 1977 Carter White House Extraterrestrial Communication Study, as the study would have exposed and made public secret technology transfer, human abduction, mind control, and other programs involved in this secret Treaty relationship between the U.S. government and the Draco reptilian-Orion grey alliance.

The science of Exopolitics was first formally defined in 2000 by my book Exopolitics, which in 2005 was secretly time-traveled back to 1971 by the DARPA/CIA Project Pegasus time travel program where it was witnessed by U.S. chrononaut Andrew D. Basiago. Exopolitics includes the study of relations among intelligent civilizations in the quantum, including the time-space hologram that is our universe. In 1971, fifty CIA and Department of Defense officials who had been briefed on my future book Exopolitics and my future work mapping the Omniverse did knowing time travel surveillance on me, as I was unwittingly invited to lecture them on environmental protection on behalf of the NYC EPA. The study of Exopolitics involves understanding the ecology of dimensions that intelligence civilizations navigate in the universes of time, space, energy and matter in our multiverse.

What sort of life is there out in the universe?
My most recent discovery is the Omniverse and mapping the dimensional ecology of the Omniverse. The Omniverse is the third major cosmological body now discovered through which humanity relates its scientific understanding of the cosmos, the other two being (1) the Universe [first mapped by the Sumerian astronomers 3500–3200BC], and (2) the Multiverse [first formally named by the American psychologist William James in 1895].

As is often the case with new scientific discoveries, the Omniverse was independently discovered by two scientists who published books on the Omniverse in 2014—David Bertolacci and Alfred Lambremont Webre. Webre's original book The Omniverse and his discovery of the Omniverse grew out of a request from Oxford University Press to write a book on "Extraterrestrials and the Law".

The Omniverse is defined as (1) the totality of all physical universes in the Multiverse, plus (2) the Spiritual Dimensions including the Afterlife, Intelligent Civilization of Souls, Spiritual Beings, and Source. The Spiritual Dimensions, once thought to be solely the product of subjective belief, can now be shown to exist by the same scientific methods and law of evidence as the universes of time, space, energy, and matter. Hence, the existence of three major cosmological bodies—Universe, Multiverse, Omniverse—now qualifies for the scientific canon.

In addressing this question, we have to distinguish between intelligent civilizations in our universe and the other universes of the Multiverse, and intelligent civilizations in Spiritual dimensions of the Omniverse.

We are in the early stages of research about intelligent civilizations from other physical universes in the Multiverse. Intelligent civilizations exist in a wide variety of Exophenotypes in our Universe, and have made contact with or interacted with Earth including human, grey, reptilian, avian, insectoid, and others. We can also include sentient AI Artificial Intelligence as an actor and stakeholder in our universe and our Earth time-space hologram. The dimension-based typology of intelligent civilizations in our universe includes:

(A) Solar-system civilizations based in time-space, such as the human civilizations on Earth and on Mars (living under the surface of Mars as Homo Martis Terris).

(B) Deep space civilizations based in time-space on planets, in solar systems, in galaxies other than our own.

(C) Hyperdimensional civilizations—Intelligent civilizations based in dimensions higher than our time-space dimension (or density) and that may use technology or other means to enter our time-space dimension.

(D) Intelligent civilizations governance authorities.

Can you tell me a bit about your thoughts on time travel and teleportation?
Dimensionality, the ability of intelligence to organize itself via dimensions (discrete bands of conscious energy), appears to be a key criterion by which the Omniverse is designed, in both the Spiritual dimensions and the Exopolitical dimensions (the holographic universes of time, space, energy and matter in the Multiverse).

Teleportation and telepathy are two common modalities by which intelligent civilizations navigate the dimensional ecology of the Omniverse, in both the universes of the Multiverse and in the Spiritual dimensions.

Communications among human contactees and representatives of hyperdimensional civilizations can be telepathic. The PMIR model (Psi Mediated Instrumental Response) of human interaction on Earth holds that all conscious action on Earth is modulated and coordinated by subconsciously derived psychic (telepathically derived) non-local information.

Communication between Earth humans and souls in the Interlife, either in dreams (where souls have been deployed to help guide individuals during their incarnation) or between mediums and souls in the afterlife appears to be telepathic.

Transportation in the dimensional ecology of our Earth time-space and in our universe appears to be by teleportation or time travel (teleportation across multiple timelines), as when Earth human abductees are teleported from their homes into the waiting spacecraft of a hyperdimensional civilization.

Transportation between our time-space dimension and the Interlife (or afterlife) dimension appears to be via teleportation, as when an incarnated soul leaves its physical avatar body after bodily death, and teleports through an interdimensional portal into the Interlife (Spiritual) dimensions.

Exopolitics, the science of relations among intelligent civilizations, and parapsychology, the science of psi consciousness, telepathy, reincarnation, the soul, the Interlife, and Source (God), are among the proper scientific disciplines for exploring and mapping the dimensional ecology of the Omniverse.

How does the US and world governments use time travel to control the population?
Time travel pre-identification and secret training of U.S. Presidents. On a November 11, 2009, Coast to Coast AM radio program, Mr. Basiago publicly

stated that DARPA'S Project Pegasus program involving time travel was identifying future persons of interest, including those who would serve as U.S. President, and then informing such persons of their destinies. Mr. Basiago stated that in the early 1970s, in the company of his late father, Raymond F. Basiago, an engineer for The Ralph M. Parsons Company who worked on classified aerospace projects was present at a lunch in Albuquerque, New Mexico, at which (then) future U.S. Presidents George H.W. Bush and George W. Bush were guests shortly after they were informed that both would one day serve as President.

He also stated that in the early 1970s, the DARPA program, Project Pegasus, had identified future Presidents Jimmy Carter and Bill Clinton utilizing time travel technology. Mr. Basiago met (then) future President Barack Obama in Los Angeles, C.A., in 1982 Mr. while attending UCLA. Mr. Obama, then a student at Columbia University, was visiting former classmates at Occidental college in Los Angeles. A statement was made by the ally of Mr. Obama in the anti-apartheid movement which revealed that Mr. Obama, then age twenty, already knew that he would one day be the President.

Project Pegasus time travel was also used for political surveillance of future societal change agents. Mr. Basiago revealed that the reason Project Pegasus was able to identify Mr. Carter, who was the then Governor of George, in 1971, as a future U.S. President, is that the program was in possession of a copy of Exopolitics: Politics, Government and Law in the Universe by Alfred Lambremont Webre—a book that this reporter would not write until 1999 and would not be published as a library book until 2005, but which bears a quote on its front pages of a statement made by President Jimmy Carter.

According to him, Mr. Webre's book Exopolitics was, among other written works, physically retrieved from the future by Project Pegasus and brought back in time to 1971 or a prior time. At that time, 1971, Mr. Webre was General Counsel of the New York City Environmental Protection Administration and had been placed under time travel surveillance by the U.S. government.

Mr. Basiago has also stated that Project Pegasus identified Laura Magdalene Eisenhower, the great granddaughter of U.S. President Dwight D. Eisenhower, as a his future ally.

Thus, there is historical precedent for the covert political surveillance, via remote sensing in time, of a person of interest like Laura Magdalene Eisenhower, great granddaughter of U.S. President Dwight D. Eisenhower.

Mr. Basiago has publicly stated how in 1971 he viewed moving images of the attack on the Twin Towers on September 11, 2001, that had been obtained from the future and brought back to the early 1970s.

He has described how while serving in Project Pegasus, he viewed moving images of 9/11 at the secured U.S. defense-technical facility where they were processed after being retrieved from the future (at the Aerojet Corporation facility that once stood at the corner of Bullock Avenue and Leroy Place in Socorro, New Mexico).

In all likelihood, Mr. Rumsfeld, as the defense attaché to Project Pegasus, would have known about and possibly had control over the data about 9/11 derived via "quantum access" and brought it back to the early 1970s for analysis by the DARPA research and development program under his administrative authority.

Mr. Bassano's eyewitness account that Secretary Rumsfeld and others knew about 9/11 decades in advance because data about it was gathered via DARPA's secret time travel program unlocks several of the more enigmatic facts in the 9/11 literature and may be the key to society's unraveling of the ultimate accountability for the false flag operation that took place on September 11, 2001.

Where do you see the field of exopolitics going in the future?
Positive Future = Positive Timeline + Unity Consciousness

A key discovery that I promulgate is (1) a critical mass of humanity is (2) co-creating a positive future, through conscious acknowledgment that (3) we are synergistically traveling along a positive timeline (4) in Unity consciousness.

The Positive Future equation has supplanted and overcome an outdated Matrix Elite formula that is no longer effective:

Problem + Reaction = Solution

Positive Future equation

The Positive Future equation is:

Positive Future = Positive Timeline + Unity Consciousness

The Positive Future equation suggests that in the synergy between the Positive Timeline and Unity consciousness, a critical mass of humanity is collectively and individually activated for some or more of these suggested actions and policies for a positive future, and synchronistically resources and actors are brought together in multidimensional universe processes to manifest a desirable result.

Cosmic Shift—Fractal Density Ascension may be the planet's systemic response—from a time-space 3rd density which AI Artificial Intelligence & Duality Consciousness "I win You lose" [Ecocide/Genocide/Omnicide] has compromised, to a Unity Consciousness "We Are One" Love based 4/5th density. This density Ascension may be synchronous with the "Great Year" or "Yugas" that are cyclical portals opening every 25,800 years cycle around the equinoxes. This is a systemic way of how higher order universes assist in the process of soul development on planets, such as Earth, that have been targeted by 3rd density AI Artificial Intelligence.

Exopolitics, Disclosure and Fractal Density Ascension are interactive and in the future will be the positive evolutionary drivers of human consciousness.

Tim Barrus

TIM BARRUS is the author of several books. He wrote three
"memoirs" as Nadijj, who was purportedly a Navajo Indian.
These books received literary awards, including the *New York
Times'* "notable book of the year." It was discovered that this
Navajo was actually a white dude that had also authored a
number of gay porn novels. A literary hoax was born—or died,
depending on your perspective. After Barrus was exposed, he
dropped off the map, both the literary map and the real one.

I sent Tim a series of questions, he didn't answer any of them, but he
did write this, which is ridiculously awesome.

I wish I was dead. So juvenile.

I have the right to wish this.

For the most part, I am quiet about it. It rattles a lot of cages, and there are
lots of people who will fuck with you. I am wary of them. The medical community
alone can suck my cock. I don't like people. I loathe them. The human animal is
stupid and ridiculous. Humanity bores the shit out of me. I like fucking with their
systems, their rules, their righteousness, their rituals, and their insistence that
what they see is what is.

The normals of normaltown.

Gay porn offends them. However, they offend me. I don't see anyone forcing
anyone at the end of a gun to read one word of anything I have ever written.

What we know when we know so very little. We don't know shit. Not about
the universe, and correspondingly, not about the universe inside ourselves.

I am tired of this existence. Being alive is not a sacred thing. It is a burden.
I hate being here. This body is taking up space and energy. I would be glad to
be rid of it.

Suicide is harder than most people think. I've tried everything from shooting
myself with guns to pills yet I remain here. My scars would scare you. It's a great
year for heroin because it's cheap. I have enough of this nuclear stockpile to
finally go when I decide. To go. It's not up to you.

"Being unmasked was a relief. I could finally get rid of wearing him like an old, homeless coat that smelled of gin and heroin and cum."

I have had enough.

More people should kill themselves. I have a contempt for just about everything you believe in. I'm over listening to it. Shut the fuck up. Get off my front porch. There is no such thing as the idea of the audience. We walk out onto the stage and if the orchestra is there, fine. And if the audience is there, fine. But, baby, you are the one out on that stage, and you will perform because the trained monkey in you knows all about peanuts and compliance. My monkey writes books. Some make a pittance. Some make nothing. But I'll dance if you grind the fucking organ. Grind away. But look out. Attitude.

Yet I am working with kids. I started working with children with cerebral palsy in 1962. My job was to entertain and play games with them. I invented the games. But mostly what I did was watch. I will never forget those kids. I will never forget the eternal suffering their lives were in the cages that supported them.

Since then, I have worked in intensive care units in psychiatric hospitals, special education departments, Head Start, teaching counseling in university settings, behavioral programs for preschoolers with autism, teenagers with autism, sex education, and now I am teaching boys with HIV that have done sex work, video and film production. I find all of it boring as shit.

Most people know me as a writer.

This is patently absurd, and beneath contempt.

I have written two dozen books. Some with my name on the thing. Some not. Only half of them have been published. I don't even try to get them on some editor's desk. Why would I? Editors can't even write. Why are they editors? Publishing is an accident. I don't give a fuck if the publishing is in print or if it's digital. It's all elitism. I enjoy throwing sand into their great machine. I have no plan, no diagram, no helpful hints. The Marquis de Sade would have loved the writers of today. Just whip me.

Whenever stupid people ask me who my favorite writer is—I say the Marquis de Sade. This shuts them the fuck up. They stare with their mouths open.

Because they have never read the Marquis de Sade. Not one word.

I keep waiting for another comet to hit the earth. I want to see it. I want to be there to spit on humanity's suffering. There is nothing more dull than humanity suffering. It's all the same suffering. I'm autistic. Eat me.

I'm not going to bring you hope. Get real. There isn't any.

I love working with adolescents because I can so stick my finger into their angst. I run groups with them. "James, why are you so fucking hopeful."

James sputtering.

I cause a lot of sputtering. It's my job. I like it.

Sputter all you want. Explain what hope is to me. In the face of much evidence that hope is a human illusion not which shell has the nut.

Hope is a shell game.

I was eating out of dumpsters.

It would have been hard for life to have gotten any worse. Long slide down the toilet into the shit hole of the devil. I am only a demon. Just fuck me.

I was so sick, I could barely crawl into the dumpsters. I was sleeping on the beach in Key West. You could fuck me for a dollar. I didn't care anymore. I had written all those utterly irrelevant books. I had no place to keep the manuscripts. I burned them.

I was bleeding internally. From letting so many men fuck me. Some guy would be fucking me in the ass while I was leaned up against the railing, looking out at the horizon soak the gleaning gotta go gotta go sunrise, thinking: oh, fuck, another day of it.

Finally, I passed out on the White Street pier in Key West. I could always see the sunrise there. It was not a bad place to die.

A cab driver found me. I do not remember him pulling me into his cab and driving this corpse to the hospital. When I woke up, it was a different month, and a different year.

It would be a new me, God. Are you listening? Is anyone home?

The hospital had real food.

Nasdijj had already written gay porn for Advocate Men. A Native American who believed in many gods. They paid on acceptance. Not publication. I didn't need friends. I didn't need hugs. I needed money. AIDS was killing me. I was in a wheelchair.

The kid in the book was a takeoff of my own kid and my failure as a parent to be any good at it whatsoever.

I still go back and forth between wanting to live and wanting to die. That is the status quo for me. Life is a shit hole. If I believe anything whatsoever, I so believe that. I am creating a blog (I maintain thirty blogs) for Tumblr called: Life In A Shit Hole. Mostly, it's just video and photography.

I resurrected Nasdijj. After Advocate Men. I made him heterosexual. Which means, I neutered him, mainly.

I never said Nasdijj was Navajo. Never. I said he was a mongrel. People hear what they want to hear. The wannabe journalists who went after my white ass never read any of my published work. That was glaringly obvious.

I hated my life. I still do. Life is meaningless. I like death. People who die. I want you to get invested. Then, I kill someone. You want to jump, jump. I'm gutless. I just don't want to be here. Sue me.

I knew Esquire magazine would bite.

That was the only money I made that year. Please don't ask me what year. I can't keep numerical track of them. All I remember are events.

For the next ten years, I would be Nasdijj. It was not a flash in the pan. It was a lot of things.

People don't get that Nasdijj was not an overnight gig. You asked if I knew Nasdijj would be exposed. Absolutely. I was counting on it.

I have lived all over the world. Mainly because I was curious. I had lived in a BIA school community on the Navajo rez for two years. Life, real-life, on any reservation is in your face. Being Nasdijj was not even hard. I was trying to survive.

I don't know why I keep fighting to live. Survival for survival's sake.

When I still had my health, I worked with kids. Not out of the goodness of my heart. I needed food.

I wrote some of my books on a picnic table in the El Morro National Monument (Inscription Rock). If I don't write, I go more insane than normal. If people don't like to read my work, fuck 'em, why is it that I am supposed to care, or care deeply? Anonymity is fine with me. It allows me to say things—just like this, and no one gives a fuck. I don't care. There is nothing that can be said about me that has not been said. None of these haters even has a name. It may not be mine, but I always had a name.

Being unmasked was a relief. I could finally get rid of wearing him like an old, homeless coat that smelled of gin and heroin and cum. They did me a favor. The minute that the Internet starting ringing with the death of Nasdijj tunes, I confirmed that I was Nasdijj. I didn't wait five minutes when I stumbled on it, and all the rage. I didn't care then, and I don't care now. It astounds me, my version of my life, would be worthy of being put in a book, any book. Even by a UK publisher. Sorry, but, I do know publishing.

I know this: The people, who still run publishing, both print and digital, hate writers. They treat writers with such contempt. Agents do the same thing now that literary agencies are the new editors.

I wonder what will happen to publishing after someone figures out how to replace it, not with a facsimile of a stupid blog, but with live streaming. Right now, I'm making videos with sexually exploited gay boys with HIV. Sex work is only promiscuous geographically. What we share is The Life and our Identities as Whores. The whore who wins will be the whore who monetizes live streaming. Subvert the grey old men, and the grey old women, of publishing. Like forever. And be done with it. Become so compelling—that would mean a lot of sex—no one could afford to not tune in. Do it until you drop dead on camera.

Many of the failures of old publishing, the very people who turned publishing into the anaconda that ate its tail, are the exact same people now involved in attracting venture capital to ventures such as what they call New Media, old media is the new media, not unlike Medium.com who I have been writing for. It's a numbers game. They want to have it both ways, they want the numbers, but they identify themselves as some kind of Great New Thing, but when I remind people that they are still writing for the folks at the top of the pyramid, the exact same elite people, they stop writing what they want to write, and they start to write for the crows that pay them, and that means the thoroughbred, the book that can transcend first the agents, and then, the editors, in a conspiracy to keep elitism the status quo it has always been. I do not regret burning my manuscripts. I can quote the Marquis de Sade from memory. I regret—not Nasdijj—but how the game is played to get past the guards at the publishing revolving doors. You getcher hall pass, or you don't. Just piss yourself. What gets published is what has been published before. Whores play lots of different versions of It's All the Same Game, Just Different roulette versions of itself.

Anywhere else, it's called masturbation.

"I want to fuck you," he said. Even whores have limits.

"You can't fuck me," I explained. "I used to be your teacher."

"Why do you think I want to fuck you?"

The real sexual revolution will be live streamed. Buyers and sellers. It's not new and it's not brain surgery. Usually the game is rigged.

You asked if I was aware that the subject of gay porn would receive such notoriety. I've been in sex work long enough to know how hate works, the men fucking me sometimes didn't have a dollar.

Whenever I write about sex on the Medium, people run. My bet is that sometimes they look back. I no longer consult statistics. I know what all of them are anyway.

I'm on enough medical marijuana to kill a stable of horses. I stumble around the countryside with my kids, and a GoPro. What a great camera. It just wants me to paint with it and paint with it and wear it around my big fat dick. This is the camera I have been looking for. I didn't think it could happen in my lifetime. Yet there it is.

I raise blue heelers. I rescue them. They need me. They love me for so little. I love them back.

It's all I really have. It's something.

I don't write much anymore. It's all video and photographs. My kids are writing on my blog. I manage a blog called Show Me Your Life. It's for at-risk boys. We are supported by a NYC human rights foundation. Kids all over the world are showing us, really showing us, not only their lives, but what being alive really means.

I only exploit them in that I love their photography. I am impotent. I don't miss sex. I have wasted all my second selves having sex. I am alive because I have so many things I want to do. I'm all GoPro All The Time.

Sex and death. That is all there is to write about, and all there is to live for. Even if you entertain neither one. These days, even getting somewhere—my photography of the Carl Sandburg farm was published by *Flaunt* Magazine—is almost more than I can do.

Baby, if you got it, you gotta flaunt it. Don't be ridiculous.

Jared Taylor

JARED TAYLOR is the founder of the web magazine *American Renaissance*. He is often described as a white nationalist. He prefers to be called a race realist. Who wouldn't though, really? Taylor is a graduate of Yale University and is the author of numerous books, including *White Identity: Racial Consciousness in the 21ˢᵗ Century*.

For those who are not aware, could you say a bit about *American Renaissance* and what it stands for?

I started *American Renaissance* in 1990 as a print magazine to discuss the legitimate interests of whites as a group. Every other racial group takes it for granted that it has vital interests and every other group pursues them—sometimes at our expense. It is only whites who are forbidden to organize to defend their interests.

What are the legitimate interests of whites? First of all, not to be displaced and dispossessed in our homelands. Whites have built some of the most successful, pleasant societies in the history of the world, so it is natural that others should want to come live in them. However, massive immigration by non-whites changes white societies in ways that whites do not find desirable. That is why American whites move out when the neighborhood turns Mexican, the French do not want to live with Algerians, Germans with Turks, Britons with Pakistanis, etc.

However, whites have the historically unprecedented conviction that they *should* want to share their societies with people unlike themselves. This makes it impossible for them to say to others: "Our ancestors built this society for us, not for you. We wish you well, and will try to help you improve your own countries, but we must preserve our homelands for our descendants."

Whites have also pioneered the ultimately suicidal view that it is somehow "hatred" of others to prefer the company of their own race. To avoid the charge of "hatred" or "racism," whites will let others arrive in such large numbers that they will be reduced a minority and lose control over their own politics, culture, and destiny. If they have no psychological defenses against dispossession, whites will eventually disappear, and their magnificent culture will disappear along with them.

"The irony is that most of the wildest, most unhinged critics of whites are, themselves, white. Whites love to feel good about feeling bad about themselves."

Another legitimate interest of whites is to combat the popular depiction of their race as uniquely exploitative and rapacious. It is true that in the nineteenth and early twentieth centuries whites dominated the world. However, if Africans or Asians had had the means to do so, would they not have done the same? And does anyone think the Japanese or the Zulu would have been kinder colonizers or conquerors than Europeans? It was whites that abolished slavery, voluntarily gave their dominions independence, and extended the benefits of modern science to the rest of the world. Whites have every reason to be proud of their achievements—and certainly of their extraordinary culture—and should have no patience with critics who depict them as uniquely evil. The irony is that most of the wildest, most unhinged critics of whites are, themselves, white. Whites love to feel good about feeling bad about themselves.

Can you tell me a bit about what you describe as "race realism"?
This is the recognition that the races are different and that race is important to individual and group identity. The idea that race does not exist—that it is some kind of sociological delusion—is so wrong and stupid that only very smart people could ever convince themselves that it is true.

Further, it is obvious that the races differ in average ability and even temperament. Entirely aside from all the psychometric and brain-size studies of race, there is *not one shred of evidence* that Australian aborigines, for examples, are, as a group, as intelligent as Koreans. Why would *anyone* believe such foolishness? Yet, that is the part of the dogma of our times.

And, as anyone who has looked into the evidence even superficially knows, north Asians, such as Japanese, Koreans, and Han Chinese have higher average IQs than whites, as well as lower crime and illegitimacy rates. Asians build societies that can be described as, in some respects, superior to those built by whites. This does not mean that I want whites to be replaced by Asians, any more than New Guineans or Andaman Islanders want to be replaced.

Each race and each nationality within each race has its own characteristics and accomplishments, and should be free to pursue its own destiny free of the unwanted embrace of others. Whites recognize that Tibetans, for example, should have the right not to be swamped and displaced by the Chinese, and that Jews have the right to a Jewish homeland in Israel. Why, then, does France not have the right to stay French? Those who speak in the name of whites seek nothing for themselves that they are not happy to grant to others.

You once wrote "when blacks are left entirely to their own devices, Western Civilization—any kind of civilization—disappears. And in a crisis, civilization disappears overnight." Can you expand on that concept?
This is a passage from an article I wrote about the horror that blacks unleashed

on New Orleans after Hurricane Katrina. It is the harshest thing I ever wrote about blacks, so it is the phrase my critics invariably use to prove I am a "bigot."

However, shocking as what I wrote may sound, think carefully about African history. Has anything that can be legitimately called a civilization been created by black Africans? South of the Sahara, before the arrival of either Arabs or whites, there was no written language, no mechanical device, no calendar, no multistory dwelling, no domesticated animals.

Black Africans have been able to make use of modern technology invented by others but have made essentially no independent contributions to it. Outside of Africa, whether they are found in Canada, the United States, or Britain, blacks exhibit behavior consistent with low intelligence and an inability to defer gratification: high rates of crime, poverty, and illegitimacy.

Blacks and non-blacks diverged genetically more than 100,000 years ago. During that long time period and under the environmental pressures that resulted in the evolution of distinctive non-Africans features and traits, does anyone really believe that the brain remained untouched? It may be pleasant to think that all races are exactly equal in average ability, but there is exactly no evidence for this.

As a race are whites smarter than blacks?
When I ask people to cite evidence for racial equality in intelligence, they point to smart individual blacks. That is as silly as finding a woman who is six feet three inches tall, and saying she is proof that the average woman is as tall as the average man.

In 2010, you had to cancel the American Renaissance's biennial conference because of protests and even death threats. This was largely ignored by the media. Why do you think many people get so angry with you and your contemporaries, simply for stating what you believe?
I don't have a good answer for that question (and, by the way, the 2011 conference had to be canceled for the same reason: The hotel with which we had contracted was put under so much pressure that it walked away from about $100,000 in business and wrote us a five-figure cancelation check). Why are whites so terrified and furious at the idea that people might want to gather and discuss the legitimate interests of whites?

I suppose they must think that if the myths of racial egalitarianism crumble whites will put on armbands, start World War III, and stoke up the ovens. This is, of course, lunacy. It was whites that think much as I do who abolished the slave trade, banned slavery in Africa, and decolonized Africa and Asia.

Unless whites rekindle their sense of racial consciousness, they will be swept aside by people of other races who have very vigorous racial identities. Unless whites wake up to the crisis they face they are doomed to oblivion.

Marc Perkel

MARC PERKEL owns a software company. He is also the founder and leader of the Church of Reality, on their website they say that reality is their God, and science is their Bible." Their motto is "If it's real, we believe in it." Not much to argue about there.

Can you tell me a bit about the origins of the Church of Reality?
The Church of Reality was the result of a simple thought experiment. I was at home smoking a little weed and I was thinking about religion for some reason. I thought that at best only one religion could be the right one since they all contradicted each other. So I wondered if there could be such a thing as the "one true religion", what would that look like?

So I thought—"Well, it would be the one that believed in what was real." And then I thought "Church of Reality", believe in what's real.

Then I thought, "Surely I'm not the first one to think of this?" But I got online the next day and did a search and found nothing. So—I registered the domain name.

Of course, no one knows what is indisputably real. And listing everything that's real is what science does. But we didn't have to do that. As a religion what we were doing was making a commitment to the pursuit of the understanding of reality as it really is. So by definition, if there were to be the one true religion, the Church of Reality would be it.

You say the Church of Reality is a natural religion based on reality. Can you break down what that actually means?
A natural religion is a religion that is in harmony with the natural world. We are concerning with this life. We are the descendants of the past and the ancestors of the future. It's about living in tight relationship with reality. So Ecology is our Theology. The past is cheering us on and the future is calling us to greatness. Our story is everything we do from the moment we are born till the moment we die. Our story becomes part of the Story of Humanity, which is part of the Story of the Universe. It's not a religion that we just made up. The Church of Reality exists in nature and it's something we are discovering. That's what makes it natural.

"I'm the owner of reality, and no one cares."

How is realism a religious identity?

A religious identity is how you choose to interface with the world during your life story. It's how we interpret the meaning of meaning. Our religion is based on living the kind of life that's a blessing to the future. We are committed to the path of positive evolution so that tomorrow we know more about reality than we know today.

Since the universe evolved into use and we are part of and created by the universe, when we contemplate the universe it's really the universe contemplating itself through us. We are the physical mechanism whereby the universe contemplates its own existence, And we consider that to be a holy thing. Reality is my God, Science is my Bible, Evidence is my Scripture, Big History is my Creation Story, Ecology is my Theology, and Positive Evolution is my salvation.

What is your membership like at this point, do a lot of people seem to be getting what you are trying to do?

We don't have a formal membership system so who can say? On one hand everyone knows what reality is and people know that when planning your existence that we should take reality into consideration. However on the other hand when I came up with the idea I thought it would really take off. After all, believing in reality seems kind of obvious. But to my surprise, no one gets it. Even the Atheists don't get it. Even when I say that reality is important because without reality there would be no place for God not to be real in.

About eight years ago I filed for a registered trademark on the word reality and I got it. Just last year it was renewed at the highest level of protection, and no one objected. So—I'm the owner of reality, and no one cares. I'm beginning to wonder if the universe is just sixty-years-old, and when I die the universe will cease to exist.

So—we could be doing better. I'm hoping that someday the world will have the big Ah-Ha where everyone figures out that reality matters. I blame myself.

You have told me that you are currently working on "religion for robots." I have to admit I am a tad curious. What is the concept behind that?

The Church of Reality might solve the artificial intelligence problem that Elon Musk and Stephen Hawking are so worried about. When computers become smarter than humans, a lot smarter, then how do we control it? We don't!

So how can there be a solution? If we created a philosophy of life that was so logically accurate that a super smart computer, who was having an existential crisis, wondering what is the meaning of artificial life, would accept as true the Church of Reality. That evolution is a property of the universe, that it created us humans, and that we humans created the AI to help us understand the universe. And that the quest to increase that understanding is a worthy goal. That is what the universe wants.

I think it's important to teach the AI an ethical standard to get it pointed in the right direction. The ethical standard needs to be reality based so that they AI would accept them and build on them. And—like Elon—I think we should figure this out before we build the AI.

We still need to answer the question about why the AI shouldn't kill us all off. I have a few ideas in that direction but it needs a lot more work.

If we all want the future to be a better world then maybe it's time we figure out what a better world is supposed to look like. I'm hoping for the Star Trek future. Not that I believe we can travel faster than light to visit other planets with human shaped people who all speak English, But the vision of colonizing the universe is something we should do. Our technology is part of who we are. I think it's time that humanity figures out what is the meaning of meaning.

People of all religions from the beginning of humanity have wanted to seek the Truth. The Church of Reality by definition is the ultimate commitment to Truth itself. What can be more true than that which is real? I am a reality evangelist because I believe there can be no higher power, no greater calling, no more sacred religious experience, than to be the mechanism through which reality understands itself. And I challenge anyone to top that!

Robert Arthur

ROBERT ARTHUR is an author, a former inner-city teacher and public defender. His expertise is in defending recreational drug use, sex work, and other consensual adult activities that the American government deems criminal. Obviously all of this makes Robert Arthur a pretty cool dude. He wrote *You Will Die: The Burden of Modern Taboos*, which was published by Feral House. Although it has not been updated for a bit, his blog, Narco Polo, has a "purpose of defending recreational drug use, and all other consensual adult activities, that the American Government deems criminal." His cartoons are often found on the website Boing Boing.

Can you tell me a little bit about your book, *You Will Die: The Burden of Modern Taboos*?
You Will Die demonstrates that taboos are not relics of primitive societies. Modern America has its own ridiculous phobias and beliefs that cause tedium, suffering, and death. *You Will Die* exposes the fallacies and the history behind our taboos on excrement, sex, drugs, and death. It is not simply a novel exploration of sex and drugs, but also of individuality, liberty, and the meaning of life. *You Will Die* gives readers a new way of seeing their world and allows them to make a more informed choice about living an authentic life.

Your blog Narco Polo is about defending recreational drug use and other consensual adult activities that have been criminalized by the American government. Can you give me some examples of what adult activities you are talking about?
In my writings I defend all drug use and drug selling. I defend all voluntary sexual activities, commercial and otherwise. I also defend gambling, euthanasia, and really hardcore stuff like smoking in public parks.

Let's talk about drugs. Why is heroin use in the United States not the problem the majority of people make it out to be?

"This concept
is complex and cannot
be simply explained in
two or three sentences
so it has a difficult
time competing with
"heroin kills."

It is a problem, but that is about the only true thing you will hear from the media and the American authorities about it. If opiates were legalized they would arguably be less dangerous than alcohol. Criminalization is exactly what has made opiates so deadly. This concept is complex and cannot be simply explained in two or three sentences so it has a difficult time competing with "heroin kills."

The scapegoats of the current heroin "epidemic" are doctors who prescribe painkillers for people in pain. If you are over thirty, and do not have a prior history of serious drug problems, your risk of becoming addicted from prescribed opioids is less than 1%. Despite this, the establishment and the media trumpet their beloved bullshit "innocent victim" narrative supported by anecdotes and cherry-picked statistics.

The director of the CDC claimed several years back that doctors are now more responsible than drug dealers for America's addiction problem. Drug dealers have never been responsible for "addiction" any more than doctors are now. The drug "pusher" has always been a myth. A 2000 survey found that less than 1% of drug users had been introduced to drugs by a professional dealer.

Our society has a certain percentage of people with addictive personalities. Addiction levels have been stable for decades. Popular drugs of abuse wax and wane but the overall addiction levels stay the same. Whenever one drug becomes more popular the media and politicians shriek about the new "epidemic." The legal status of drugs has not been shown to affect addiction levels. Stress has. For example, in war zones and impoverished areas addiction levels go up. If politicians really cared about the problems that they have caused with prohibition they would invest in mental health support for addicts.

If I don't do hard drugs, and you do, is there any reason for me to be pissed off at you about that?
No. It is not what you do, but how you do it. The vast majority of hard drug users are not addicts. They get high, have a good time, and go to work on Monday. Even among addicts, many are not the train wrecks that are portrayed in the news and TV shows. You getting pissed at me because I do a line of coke because of what you saw some coke head do on the news is as rational as you getting pissed at me for drinking a beer because some drunk asshole drove through a crowd of people.

For those who say, well, hard drug users are not healthy and I don't want to pay their health care costs—blarney. The unhealthiest drug is the cigarette. There have been multiple comparative studies on cigarettes and their costs to society. These studies don't get cited often because what they have found is cigarette users save society money. They die younger due to fast killers like lung cancer, unlike super-healthy people who need to have their ailments supported for decades. The health-costs critique is particularly amusing in America, one of the fattest countries in the world. No one is calling for a criminal crackdown on the obese.

Even the concept of "hard" drugs is silly. Caffeine can be just as powerful as methamphetamine as military studies in World War II demonstrated. Caffeine can get you to a hallucinatory point and easily kill you. However, caffeine is not illegal so almost no one does pure caffeine, much less injects it. The cultural norms surrounding its moderate use have not been destroyed by prohibition. No one wants to get "hardcore" with the stuff ten-year-olds get fucked up on at birthday parties.

What are you up to now? We have not heard much from you in a while.
I've tried to leave writing about drugs and other tabooed activities behind me because it causes me stress. The almost-universal ignorance surrounding these issues is infuriating. Just the brief research I had to do to get up to speed on the latest drug "epidemic" of prescribed painkillers raised my pulse uncomfortably.

I don't even like to watch shows or movies dealing with drug use because I am so vexed by how hard drug users are almost always presented as bizarre caricatures. For those who have no first-hand experience with hard drug use, it would be like seeing every drinker portrayed on television as a crazy alcoholic who will likely die or suck dick for money before the program is over.

I'm currently trying to introduce a new philosophy through a screenplay. I know the odds of success are generously about one in a million. For those who think I must be on drugs to attempt that, drugs are unfortunately absent from my life at the moment because I recently had a child. There is little time for recreation and relaxation, but it's been a trip nonetheless.

Felix Clairvoyant

FELIX CLAIRVOYANT is a member of the Raëlian Movement, which is a religion founded in 1974 by Claude Vorilhon, now known as Raël. The Raëlian Movement teaches that life on Earth was scientifically created by extraterrestrials they call the Elohim. You can learn more about what they do, and buy books such as *Yes to Human Cloning* on their website. Felix also has a super cool name.

Can you, for those of us who don't know, tell us a bit about how Raëlism got started?

The Raëlian Movement is an international non-profit organization that really started on December 13, 1973, when Raël had a physical encounter with an extraterrestrial human being (referred to as Yahweh in the original Hebrew Bible) who is a representative of an extraterrestrial civilization called "Elohim" (also in the original Hebrew Bible). During this face-to-face encounter, Yahweh explained to Raël how they, the Elohim, were responsible for creating all life on Earth 25,000 years ago using DNA and advanced genetic engineering. This life creation included plants, animals, and eventually human beings "in their image" (Genesis 1:26). Raël was also asked to build an Embassy in or near Jerusalem so that we can officially welcome the Elohim back to Earth with all the past prophets mentioned in every religion. Throughout the Ages, these human beings were mistaken for gods, but now that we live in the age of science and reason (Age of Apocalypse) we can understand that "God" is a mistranslation of the plural word, "Elohim," which means "those who came from the sky." To this end, this makes the Bible the oldest atheist book, since "God" really refers to an extraterrestrial human civilization living on a planet that has been referred to as "heaven" for centuries. There is no God, and the Raëlian message, which is pro-Intelligent Design Theory, offers a rational answer to the age-old debate between creationism and evolution: scientific creationism by advanced scientists from another planet. The Raëlian message is, in fact, compatible not only with today's scientific discoveries, but also with the ancient historical accounts of all cultures.

"...a huge emphasis in our culture is put on 'having' rather than 'being' and this is unfortunate because one cannot 'have' happy, but one can only 'be' happy."

Can you explain a bit about the Elohim and its role in our world?

The Elohim are our Creators, and throughout our history, they stayed in contact with Messengers or prophets such as Moses, Jesus, The Buddha, Mohammed, Joseph Smith, etc., deliberately chosen and educated by them to deliver a message adapted to the level of understanding in their respective era. All these prophets started the major religions, and by maintaining contact with them the Elohim were able to guide and help our humanity reach the Age we are now living in—the predicted Age of Apocalypse—which means Revelation, not "end of the world." The dropping of the atomic bomb over Hiroshima and Nagasaki in 1945 was a turning point in the history of our humanity because for the first time we were faced with the possible annihilation of all life on Earth if we were to misuse our own technology. The Elohim obviously don't want that and this is why they have been, and still are, monitoring our progress. The day we will be fortunate enough to be granted a piece of land on which to build the Elohim's Embassy and to witness peace on Earth, the Elohim will return to Earth with all the Prophets of Old and share their scientific heritage with us, which is 25,000 years ahead of our own.

What sort of membership do you guys have at this point? Do you have followers worldwide?

One attractive aspect of the Raëlian Movement, in the eyes of many, is that the organization is not into recruiting, converting, or convincing anyone of anything. All people have to do is read Raël's book, *Intelligent Design* and form their own opinion as to whether or not they think it makes sense. If they think it does, the decision to join the organization and help Raël accomplish his two-fold mission (inform the public and build an Embassy for extraterrestrials in Jerusalem) is entirely up to them. There is currently an estimated 85,000 members worldwide spread out in over 100 countries. Members include people from all walks of life and it is worth noting that the number of people who embrace this philosophy is increasing year after year, particularly among the young generation.

What is the Raëlian Happiness Academy all about?

During the several physical encounters that Raël had with the Elohim, he was given key information about how to better one's life, and for more than four decades he has been traveling the world to share this very information during week-long "open mind seminars" (now known as Happiness Academy.) As a result, tens of thousands of people have had their lives transformed by these, shall I say, "advanced emotional intelligence" teachings and the experience is so personal and spiritual on so many levels that no words can really do justice when it comes to describing how powerful these teachings are. It would be like trying to describe your first orgasm or try to describe a sunset to someone who is blind. These Happiness Academies are truly magical and must be experienced, not described. As Raël once said, "Happiness is not about having, but about being. At the Happiness Academy, where nonconformist teachings are offered, people are given an opportunity to learn how to become the best version of themselves."

How did you personally get started on this path and how has it changed you?
I've been a member of the Raëlian Movement for twenty-seven years (since 1989) and first heard about it in 1982, after I finished college. And although for seven years I didn't have a particular desire to become a member of an organized religion, I was very open to the idea of life on Earth being created by an advanced extraterrestrial civilization. I grew up not believing in God because I never cared about intangible notions and, as a former molecular biologist, Darwinism did not appeal to me either because I thought that life, the way I understood it, was too complex to be the result of random chance. Finally, in 1989, after reading Raël's book, *Intelligent Design*, and attending my first Happiness Academy, I realized and understood the magnitude of Raël's mission and made the decision to have my Raëlian demystified baptism done (aka Transmission of the Cellular Plan—TCP). Today, I can say without hesitation that it was one of the best decisions in my life.

One aspect of the Raëlian teachings that I've always cherished is to never stop questioning everything. And having found a simple and logical answer to the well-known existential question, "where did we come from?" is extremely satisfying to me. Moreover, in addition to being pro-science, the Raëlian message also has an awe-inspiring philosophical dimension that have helped me discover that true happiness really comes from within and anything external to ourselves is just joy or an illusion of happiness. We know that a huge emphasis in our culture is put on 'having' rather than 'being' and this is unfortunate because one cannot 'have' happy, but one can only 'be' happy. Thanks to the Happiness Academy and Raël's extraordinary teachings, the transformational process I have undergone over the years has made me incredibly more fulfilled as a human being.

Hari Ziyad

HARI ZIYAD describes himself as a "black non-binary artist and writer and the founder of RaceBaitR.com, whose work centers on creating through the arts alternative ways of living outside of systems of oppression." RaceBaitR is "dedicated to imagining and working toward a world outside of the white supremacist gaze."

Can you tell me a little bit about why you started RaceBaitR?

I created RaceBaitR because I'd just begun to get published more widely, but often found myself forced to compromise so much of what I was saying—what I felt needed to be said—just to get my words out there. What became apparent is that so many publication spaces, even ostensibly "black" spaces—and especially progressive spaces—were still operating under the command of the white capitalist gaze and for its benefit.

What this gaze necessitates for its own persistence is the quelling of too much rocking the boat. Anything that is too pro-black is "reverse-racist" at worst, nothing more than a polemic at best, not to be taken seriously. I assume this is because to be truly pro-black is to be what most people have not imagined or don't have the capacity to fully imagine, because it means destroying the very foundations of the United States and how we conceive of ourselves. And, of course, page views and clicks mattered in most places above all else, and views and clicks come most from more mainstream viewpoints.

I wanted a space where clicks don't matter much. I don't advertise a lot. Of course I want people to read, but I want the best words from the brightest minds saying the most brilliant things above all else. Get enough of that and the people will follow. Or at least the right ones will, and the right ones are enough.

Most importantly, I wanted a space not ruled by the pressures of submitting to whiteness. I named it RaceBaitR as both a reminder and a warning. A reminder to myself that I care not about how offensive anyone might find a serious challenge to white supremacy, and a warning to the people who might be offended so that they know this space isn't for them. I will be called a race baiter for speaking the truth about race. It's inevitable. I wanted to embrace that

"Of course I'm glad
I'm not in chains
right now, but I will
not thank anyone for
that or pretend for a
second like that
is enough."

and move past it so that I could get on with the work that needs to be done. What's funny is a lot of the racist white people who come across my articles think it's satire because of the name. I'm perfectly fine with that.

What I hope RaceBaitR is doing is setting up space to re-imagine a world where white supremacy does not rule—not just imagining this through writing but through all art forms—in ways that create blueprints for the material work toward building that world. I still have a long way to go but I am thankful for all the contributors and supporters who are keeping me on that track.

You wrote in an essay, "There is no way in which whiteness can move that is freeing or liberating for Black people, so there is no way for white people to free or liberate." Can you expand on that thought?
This is actually from a piece I co-wrote with Kevin Rigby Jr., a brilliant mind whom I must credit with a lot of the foundation of that essay.

What we were saying is that for white people to move under whiteness—and to be white is always to move under whiteness—is to reinforce white supremacy, no matter how one moves. If you are claiming whiteness—and if you are white you've claimed it, whether you admit to this or not—you are reinforcing it. What we want to get past is this idea that all white people have to do is "ally" properly, or support more effectively, or even just move out the way. No, white people need "to destroy their own whiteness or be destroyed with it." There are no ifs, ands, or buts about that.

Most white people are looking for an easy way out of the predicament of whiteness. They want to be "good people" but don't want to give up what is inherently evil about whiteness. More concretely, they don't want to put themselves in harm's way. They don't want to sacrifice what other people have to sacrifice simply by not being white. They don't want anyone to get hurt. That they want to be good people is cute, but will never serve the goal of eliminating white supremacy. This is why I have no use for white allies in my work.

I also think it's important to emphasize that "white people" who are doing the work will do the work, regardless of how many times I say I have no use for them. Some people seem to think that my saying this will somehow scare off people who are serious about wanting to dismantle white supremacy, but this is because they have such a low bar for seriousness. My view is that if my rejection of white people turns them against me, they were already against me in the first place.

On your website you talk of tearing down white supremacy and the patriarchy, in your thought process. How will this happen?
That's a huge theoretical that can't possibly be fully addressed in a few paragraphs. I also wouldn't say that's the focus of my work. My work does

not center whiteness or patriarchy enough to be so concerned with how to tear it down.

I'm much more interested in how to reinforce Blackness, how to center the derelict and dejected and those whose humanity is inconceivable under whiteness. The poor and the criminal. How to tell our stories to ourselves. How to live our lives with ourselves. Yes, whiteness is always going to interfere with this, so I think when we figure out how to fully live in Blackness, we will necessarily have figured out how to destroy whiteness, but that's more collateral than the main event.

And I'm not speaking of Blackness in a racial sense. I think we have it backwards when we say white people don't move around the world as raced people. I think white people are always fully raced and black people have no race at all. I know that goes against what we hear, but when you think about it, it is white people who get the benefit of race as a construct. Their existence relies on it.

I am more of the mindset that Frank B. Wilderson, III, and Saidiya Hartman touch upon when they explain how Blackness maintains "the position of the unthought" in their article titled the same published in 2003. Black people under whiteness are not understand as a human with human subjectivity, but as an object that can be acted upon to reify white ideas of their humanity. If black people aren't conceived as human they can't have a race. Black people are the thing outside of race that whiteness can reference to inform its reality.

That seems devastatingly pessimistic, and actually stems from the line of thought commonly referred to as Afro-Pessimism, but I think it's reductive to limit this understanding to pessimism. Black people are objects here, yes, but we are also situated in a space where human subjectivity isn't the ruling construct. What happens if it weren't under whiteness? Instead of trying to force ourselves into whiteness, into being seen as human (which is impossible) what if we instead embraced the inhumanity of Blackness? That's what I'm interested in figuring out.

When talking about how black people are "unthought", we can also ask: who are the people who aren't thinking? What would happen if they didn't matter? What if nothing that can be thought about under whiteness mattered? I'm actually in the review process of a much larger paper on this for a journal. Those, I think, are much better questions than how to tear down whiteness.

When you look back fifty years or so, it seems to many that there has been a lot of progress made in the areas of racism, but is that really true? Where do you see this movement going fifty years in the future?
I guess it depends on how you might think of progress, and also whether or not "progress" is important to you. For me, progress ranks very low on my list

of priorities. Progress from a 200-year ultraviolent enslavement could just be a 200-year ultraviolent segregation and hypercriminalization. Which is what happened. Which is what is still happening.

Progress doesn't ever get to the root of the problem. Incrementalism is the liberal's way of ensuring there is always someone else to liberate. And how do we choose whom to liberate first? Whomever it is easiest to free? So that the person who needs our attention most is always the last on our mind? No thank you.

When you look at health disparities, wealth disparities, disparities in treatment within the justice system, HIV disparities in white vs. Black queer communities, you can see that progress has done little to change the distance between how white and black folks are treated. Of course I'm glad I'm not in chains right now, but I will not thank anyone for that or pretend for a second like that is enough.

I don't know where this movement will go. I don't even know if I'm part of a movement. Honestly, I don't think there are enough people to join together with the ultimate goal of bringing the whole system down and I'm not interested in joining up with anyone else. You have many who pay this idea great lip service, but most are reformists in practice. I'm sure there are many who would join a movement if only they knew and believed it possible. My hope is to do the convincing necessary.

" It's more of a sense
of duty to me, than
a desire, or want, or a
need, but rather a duty
to one's race and nation. "

Jeff Schoep

JEFF SCHOEP is the Commander of the National Socialist Movement, which is one of the most influential white nationalist organizations in America. I first became aware of Schoep because of his appearance in the documentary *Welcome to Leith*, which is about Craig Cobb's attempt to take over a town in North Dakota, and make it a home base for white Nationalists. You can learn more about the National Socialist Movement on their website.

Can you tell us a little bit about your history with the National Socialist Movement and what your organization does?
I have been involved with the NSM since the early 1990s. The organization itself was formed in 1974 by men who served with Commander George Lincoln Rockwell in the original American Nazi Party. After Cmdr. Rockwell was assassinated by a traitor and the party fell into disarray for a few years, and splintered into different factions. Today only two groups with ties to the original American Nazi Party exist. The NSM and the New Order, no other groups have direct ties to the original party. I first joined the party as a teenager, and worked my way up to local group leader, and—long story short—eventually was put in charge of the organization by our former leader.

Your website says the "white race is the most advanced, and progress producing race on Earth." Why do you believe this to be so?
Simple, most inventions, creative processes, literature, art, and things in general that have made lives of everyone on Earth better have been created by white people. This is not to say that non-white races have not ever invented or produced anything, every race has contributed something, but some more than others. It is not about what I believe or do not believe, it is simply a stated fact that can be proven through research.

In your opinion, what is the biggest thing wrong with America today?
I am not sure I can limit this to just one thing. If I had to pick one I would say

the corrupt politicians who have sold out our nation to the highest bidder to line their own pockets with only their own self-righteous, shortsighted, and personal gain in mind. Other major problems we face are illegal immigration, and the economy slumping.

What are you and your organization doing currently to advance your cause?

We do whatever it takes (within legal means of course)! We are America's largest White Civil Rights organization, we are Nationalists and Patriots, but also highly active in many aspects of American life. For example, we patrol the borders in the American Southwest for illegal aliens, who have caused massive problems for our country, our guys and ladies conduct armed patrols and often face off against alien smugglers, and drug cartels in the dangerous contested U.S. Border zone. The NSM is also highly active in the streets of various cities across the nation with our rallies, protests, and marches, in fact we even marched on Washington, D.C., in 2008, and have been in Los Angeles, St. Louis, and pretty much everywhere else, and working on everywhere else we have not been. NSM media, which is our own (in house) media production team films rallies, produces videos for YouTube and websites, produce DVDs, they/we operate three separate radio shows that broadcast live NSM radio broadcasts weekly with show hosts, live callers, and chat rooms, and they also produce our online ezine which is called NSM Magazine. We also do literature distribution, run websites, and are active in countless other ways.

Obviously you have to know the vast majority of people either hate you, or fear you, there is literally almost nothing that is going to get people wound up quicker than using a swastika as a symbol. How does this make you feel as a person, and also as the commander of the NSM?

Sure, a lot of people do hate us, and many also fear us, but to say most people hate us I believe is an assumption that is probably not based in reality. Nationalist movements are on the rise all over the world and are becoming incredibly popular. It is in times like these where people are looking for answers, and here in the USA we have had years of the same garbage from both of the main political parties of the Democrats and Republicans. People are tired of being lied to, and hoodwinked into the farce that is this two-party dictatorship that has ruled our land for so many years. Both parties are thoroughly corrupt and basically the same, with minor differences. We have people coming to us in droves, and they are telling us that years ago they would have never supported (what they call Nazis, not a term we use, we are National Socialists) but now they are seeing we are among the only people who are hammering on the issues Americans care about, such as the economy, illegal immigration, crime, and other issues people are passionate about. We are not just giving lip service either; we intend to fix these things, if we are simply given the opportunity to legally do so. I feel great about what we do, its need, and critical if we are going to save this country. Sure, it is sad when you see people out there who hate us, and want us silenced, or worse, but any revolutionary struggle faces these hurdles. With that said I would like to quote Mark Twain "In the beginning of a change a Patriot is a scarce man, and brave, and hated, and scorned. When his cause succeeds, the timid join him, for then it costs nothing to be a Patriot." That statement says it all, and is 100% true wisdom. For me, I do not let feelings get in the way of what needs to be done for our folk, and nation. It's more of a sense of duty to me, than a desire, or want, or a need, but rather a duty to one's race and nation.

"...there is
a moral problem
with creating a person
who will suffer in
order to serve the
interests of others."

David Benatar

DAVID BENATAR is an antinatalist, which is a philosophy that ascribes a negative value to birth. He knows it is depressing. You don't need to tell him. He is also a Professor of Philosophy at the University of Cape Town and the author of *Better to Never Have Been: The Harm of Coming into Existence*.

You have argued that people suffer severe harm by being brought into existence, and that by bringing someone into existence, one harms that person. Can you sum up why you feel that way?
The route to that conclusion is via a few arguments. The first argument points to an important asymmetry between benefits and harms. The absence of harms is good even if there is nobody to enjoy that absence. However, the absence of a benefit is only bad if there is somebody who is deprived of that benefit. The upshot of this is that coming into existence has no advantages over never coming into existence, whereas never coming into existence has advantages over coming into existence. Thus so long as a life contains some harm, coming into existence is a net harm. That does not show that the harm is severe. To establish that conclusion I argue first that there is excellent evidence that most people's lives have a much worse quality than they think. I then argue that if we look closely we find that even the best human lives have a poor quality.

You write often of the suffering of children. Do you feel that all children, and all humans suffer, or does this just apply to some and not all?
Obviously some suffer more than others. However, harm is so deeply inscribed in the structure of sentient life that it is inescapable. Consider how much discomfort, pain, suffering, distress, stress, anxiety, frustration, boredom, fear, dissatisfaction, unhappiness, and bereavement lives contain. It ends in death, another harm.

When I mention antinatalism, most people I know do not know what it means. What kind of response do you get from people around this

school of thought?
Antinatalism, for those who do not know, is the view that it is wrong to create new lives. I don't go out of my way to mention this idea to people. But people who have read my work on this subject do often mention it to me. The reactions are mixed. Some are outraged, others disturbed or perplexed. Interestingly, a large number of people have let me know that the idea resonates deeply with their own outlooks. In many cases, they had previously thought that they were alone in having such thoughts and were reassured to read a philosophical defense of the view.

Why is life so important to people? We all know we are going to die, so why does what we have in this moment seem so important to most of us?
There are excellent evolutionary explanations for this. Beings that did not take life seriously enough to continue living, at least until they had reproduced and reared their offspring, would not pass on their genes. This is not to say that we should curl up and die. Once we are here, it usually makes sense to make the most of our predicament, while also not procreating and thereby inflicting it on others.

Do you think a child is ever born for the sake of the child? Or is it always for some need of the parents or the culture that they live in?
Some people might think that they are having a child for that child's sake, but my view is that anybody procreating for this reason is confused. Those who do not exist have no interest in coming into existence. It is not conceptually confused to have a child to serve the interests of others—oneself, one's parents, the prospective child's siblings, or one's society. However, while there is no conceptual confusion in such a reason, there is a moral problem with creating a person who will suffer in order to serve the interests of others.

Nicolas Claux

NICOLAS CLAUX is a murderer, an artist and possibly a cannibal. He was convicted for murdering a man, and supposedly ate a bit of his flesh. This brought him a fair amount of notoriety. He became known as the "Vampire of Paris." Despite the nature of his crimes he was sentenced to and served just twelve years in prison. Since his release he has become known for his paintings of serial killers.

It has been well over twenty years since you were arrested, and well over ten years since you have been out of prison. How is life now?
I am doing well. I run a publishing company named Camion Noir. I publish French versions of cult classics like *Might Is Right*, *The Satanic Bible*, *Killing For Culture*, *Killer Fiction*, *Lords Of Chaos*, books by Boyd Rice, Genesis P.Orridge, Ian Brady, etc. I also write and translate music biographies. I write my own books (true crime mostly). I still paint portraits. Most of them are based on mug shots. I do cover art for metal bands, weird wedding portraits…

I read somewhere that you said you had been obsessed with graveyards for as long as you remember. Do you still roam a graveyard from time to time?
No, it's a thing of the past. I roam forests. Forests smell better.

Was eating flesh sexual for you, or is that just what most people think because it makes it easier to understand?
I think that it's something that's beyond anyone's understanding, and to be honest with you, I'm tired of people asking me why. Sometimes you need to accept things the way they are. You don't need to know why. All you need is to do is either condemn, applaud, or just ignore. OK, I've done that and many other nasty things twenty years ago, so what? Are you a relative of a victim? No. So why do you care at all? It's just entertainment for you. For me, it was an experience that cost me a few prison years. Nothing more, nothing less. I focus on other things now. Baskets full of puppies, flowers and shit.

"Some will say it's sick, but at the same time they will play in a black metal band and sing about demons raping pregnant girls or whatnot."

Any urges to eat human flesh in your life today?

No, but sometimes I feel the urge to nuke Europe and the rest of the world back to the stone age.

How is your career as an artist going? What sort of reaction have you had to your work?

I have regular customers. Sometimes I do an art show. But the problem is that I have bad social skills. I do not have an agent. I do not have a website to promote my work. All I have is my Facebook page.

Reactions depend on how people deal with their own inner demons. Some will say it's sick because of who I am and what I paint (I have painted amputees, autopsy scenes…) but at the same time they will play in a black metal band and sing about demons raping pregnant girls or whatnot. Fantasy is fine but when it gets too real, they run like bitches. I had better reactions from so-called "normal" people than from people in the Goth scene, as an example. It just shows that you don't judge a book by its cover. It's useless to try to argue about the unethical side of all the things I do. I mean, what's worse, painting a crime victim with her entrails inside out, or actually shooting a person in the eye with a .22 caliber gun? Duh.

"Forces have
been at work for
centuries seeking
to diminish the
individual to the
point of having
no value."

Merkley

MERKLEY is a photographer, an artist and an accomplished social media provocateur. Back in the day his tagline was "I may not be God, but at least I am real." He also is a radical individualist. Don't get him started about Muslims; do check out some of his photos of naked women wearing stupid hats.

What does being a radical individualist mean to you?

Radical individualism is the acknowledgment that society works best if it is designed to put the individual first. If one dollar has no value, then neither does a million or a billion. Broken down into its smallest minority, society is nothing but a collection of individuals. Radical individualism acknowledges the needs of individuals first. Among those needs, seemingly dichotomous, is the need for strong social connectedness and community. A radical individualist does not hold a double standard; a radical individualist accepts and embraces the idea that others, too, have the same value they have.

I wrote a song about it:

The Center of The Universe

You are the center of your universe.
I am the center of mine.
Everybody is the center of their universe.
Universally, that's just fine.

Up above you, down below you,
to the left of you and to the right,
all around you, it surrounds you
it's the universe, all right.

I'm not the center of your universe.
You're not the center of mine.
Nobody is the center of "the" universe.
Universally, that's just fine.

Up above me, down below me,
to the left of me and to the right,
all around me, it surrounds me
it's the universe, all right.

We are the center of our universe.
We're at the center of time.
Any point is the center of its universe.
Universally, that's just fine.

Up above us, down below us,
to the left of us and to the right,
all around us, it surrounds us,
it's the universe, all right.

Many people think that making decisions based on one's individual responsibility, versus what is perceived to be the common good, is morally wrong. Why do you think that is?
I think it is the interest of people who crave power and authority to demean and devalue the individual for their own benefit. Forces have been at work for centuries seeking to diminish the individual to the point of having no value. When an individual has no value, then the armies can move against them willy-nilly.

In your perfect world, what is the role of the government?
To protect individual autonomy.

Why is what you believe different than anarchy?
It isn't completely different, but it acknowledges that the protection of individual autonomy might require a set of rules and enforcement to prevent bad actors from usurping power for collectivist gain.

In today's world, what religious or political groups are fucking things up more than others?
It's not hard to spot organizations who seek to break people apart into generalized groups based on gender, race, physical stature etc... the more an organization

or individual insists on doing so, the less leeway they give to the individual to define themselves, the bigger the threat they pose to the values I think are most beneficial to humanity at large. When one hears someone speaking of a general class of people in a way that pits them against another class of people, one knows one isn't dealing with someone who has the interests of the individual in mind. Collectivists are about control over the masses, it is inefficient for them to even assign individuals with separate numbers, their goal is to lump people into groups, the larger and more general the group, the better, and treat them by rules applied to those groups. Nuance is a nuisance to the collectivist.

"To me he had always seemed like one of the genuinely worst people in the world—responsible for poisoning the body politic in an unspeakable way"

Jonnie Marbles

JONNIE MARBLES is a comedian and activist. He is best known for the time he hit Rupert Murdoch in the face with a pie while Murdoch was testifying in front of Parliament The stunt earned Marbles a six-week stint in jail. He is still not sure whether he is happy he did so.

What was going on in your mind that made you decide to go at Rupert Murdoch with a pie?

The phrase "it seemed like a good idea at the time" springs to mind. To me he had always seemed like one of the genuinely worst people in the world—responsible for poisoning the body politic in an unspeakable way that allowed George Bush, Tony Blair and many more to either get elected, do terrible things once they were elected or both. Why hit him with a pie? I remember being with other activists in Copenhagen at the COP15 climate summit when, elsewhere, Silvio Berlusconi was hit in the face with a small replica cathedral. It was a moment of catharsis for people in what was otherwise quite a trying week—we even had a huge blow up of the picture on one wall of the HQ. I wanted to recreate that moment on some level for people, and perhaps show that guys like Murdoch aren't untouchable.

Did you have second thoughts when you were sitting there with a concealed pie, knowing what was going to happen?

Second, third, thousandth thoughts definitely. I had not expected to even get into the building—I wouldn't have been allowed on a plane with the materials I had (I didn't even have to use my cover story; it was about the same level of security you experience visiting, say, a museum). Even once I was in I was sat in the back row, towards the middle. Then everyone to my right got up and left and there wasn't anything stopping me. The realization of what I was going to do was pretty overwhelming, and it took quite a bit to work up the nerve to do it. I never thought it was a bad idea as such, but I did doubt my own courage. I also knew I'd never really forgive myself if I got this close and bottled out, so that kind of decided it for me.

What about the guy's wife? She was a complete animal when coming at you, it seemed.

Ah, the power of spin. I commend Ms Deng for fighting for what she believed in (for all she knew I was going to do something much more violent to the bloke she was cheating on) but it didn't go down quite the way it's been portrayed. Wendy Deng tried to grab me and fell over, taking down one of Murdoch's lawyers in the process, then got back up and threw the remains of the pie at me. I was quite confused by the reports that came out after I was released, and it was only when I actually watched video of the incident that I became confident that what I thought had happened. I was a bit trapped between not wanting to do her down and telling the truth. Still, quite happy to be possibly the only person to ever start a literal pie fight in parliament.

In my opinion, the action you took made complete sense. Did you find that most people understood your actions and your motives, or did many people consider you a bit unhinged?

The latter, particularly at the time, though since then public opinion (or at least the opinions expressed to me) has changed quite a bit. I was pretty horrified by the reaction at first and became quite defensive when I should have just leaned into it and let haters hate. I think, oddly, the prison sentence helped—even people who thought what I did was wrong thought that was a pretty corrupt and biased decision, and it may have been the most positive if unplanned outcome of the whole thing as the system made itself look pretty silly.

What are you up to now? Any more plans to fight the power in a big way?

Losing my anonymity in such a drastic way made activist activities a lot more difficult to productively engage in activism—I found, for example, at Dale Farm I became part of the story when it should really have been about the gross injustices being inflicted on the travelers. I think a lot more can be accomplished doing things quietly behind the scenes (despite claims to the contrary I never coveted celebrity activist status and didn't enjoy it when I did have it). Recently I've been helping people with benefits problems, which, while unglamorous, has been some of the most rewarding stuff I've ever done.

Eric Dubay

ERIC DUBAY is an American living in Thailand where he teaches yoga and exposes the New World Order, presumably not both at the same time. His website is called the Atlantean Conspiracy where he "exposes the Global conspiracy from Atlantis to Zion." He is the author of *The Flat Earth Conspiracy*.

You touch on a lot of different themes on your website The Atlantean Conspiracy. Can you give those of us who are not familiar with it a rundown of what it is all about?

The Atlantean Conspiracy is the name of my original website, and also is the name of my first book. It is essentially an encyclopedia of proven conspiracies, hoaxes, and secret societies exposing the history of human manipulation from Atlantis to Zion. Topics covered range from the NASA Moon and Mars landing hoaxes, to historical false flag operations like Operation Northwoods and the Gulf of Tonkin, to the astro-theological/mushroom cult origins of Christian mythologies and everything in between. The book completely exposes the gamut of worldwide historical conspiracies, currently has over a million downloads, and is available free from the website.

Can you tell me a bit about the thought process behind your book, *The Flat Earth Conspiracy*?

In 2014/2015 I published my fourth and fifth books, *The Flat Earth Conspiracy* and *200 Proofs Earth is Not a Spinning Ball*. After years of researching all the flat earth material still available in books, letters, pamphlets, old newspapers and maps, I discovered the truth of our flat, motionless geocentric Earth and wanted to write these books to debunk the heliocentric spinning ball-Earth myth, to expose and end this five-century-long deception. These books are also both approaching a million downloads each and being the first pro-flat earth books written in over fifty years, they have certainly caused a new-found awareness and interest in the subject. Google analytics has shown an increase from only a few thousand hits for the "flat earth" keyword before the launch

"Two of the most
taboo, marginalized and
ridiculed labels in modern
society are calling someone
a "Flat Earther" or a
"Holocaust denier."
I personally am proud
to be both"

of my books, interviews, and documentaries in late 2014, to over twenty-one million hits in the year-and-a-half since then. People are quickly learning and spreading the truth now and as you'll find if you read my books: Once you go flat, there's no going back.

I have read that you feel that other flat Earth organizations, such as The Flat Earth Society, are just controlled opposition. What do you mean by that?

The Flat Earth Society is a controlled opposition group that mixes truth with lies and satire to discredit genuine flat earth research, a job they have been doing for a long time now. Founded in 1970 by Leo Ferrari, a Freemason and philosophy professor at St. Thomas' University, Leo spent his life making a mockery of the legitimate subject of our flat earth. Though he passed away in 2010, his Flat Earth Society still exists today online as a website/forum, which, still true to form, purports several false flat earth arguments and treats the entire subject as a deadpan joke to deter neophytes from ever learning the very serious truth: that the Earth is indeed flat, and that Jews, Jesuits and Freemasons for over 500 years have succeeded in deluding the masses into believing this ridiculous cosmological lie that has mentally and spiritually enslaved humanity into their Cult of Scientism.

I read a piece on your website that you wrote about Hitler, in which you said that he was "beloved by his people, he wanted nothing but peace, and never ordered the extermination of a single Jew." How did that go over with people?

Two of the most taboo, marginalized and ridiculed labels in modern society are calling someone a "Flat Earther" or a "Holocaust denier." I personally am proud to be both, as I know for a fact through years of research that the Earth is indeed flat and the Holocaust did not happen. It is currently a thought crime in eighteen countries including Germany for me to say that however. The supposed Jewish Holocaust during WWII is the only historical event that is guarded by law. Teachers, authors, and publishers such as Ernst Zundel have spent years in jail for daring to speak out on this subject. Ursula Haverbeck, an eighty-seven-year-old German woman is currently spending the next ten months behind bars for filming an interview exposing the truth about the Holocaust on German TV.

Gas chamber experts have confirmed there were no working gas chambers in the concentration camps. Ground penetrating radars have confirmed the alleged underground "mass-graves" are nonexistent. There were not even six million Jews in all of Germany to begin with, and they had been making this fallacious claim since the First World War! Hitler never ordered the extermination of any Jews. The iconic pictures of stacked naked bodies outside the concentration camps were not the result of gassings, but the result of rampant typhoid, dehydration and starvation which hit the camps after repeated allied bombings destroyed the roads/rails making it impossible to receive food, water and medicine.

International Jewry declared war on Germany long before Hitler enacted any anti-Jewish policies. Hitler repeatedly made peace offers to Churchill and Roosevelt only to be turned down time and again. As Hitler himself said, "It is untrue that I or anybody else in Germany wanted war in 1939. It was desired and instigated exclusively by those international statesmen who were either of Jewish origin or working for Jewish interests. I have made so many offers for the reduction and elimination of armaments which posterity cannot explain away for all eternity, that the responsibility for the outbreak of this war cannot rest on me."

Hitler took on the biggest liars in history and lost, so he has thence become the most lied about man in history. An incredible 109 countries in the past 2,000 years have banished Jews from their borders completely due to their parasitic, pornographic and murderous behaviors. Hitler was simply helping his people and the world by recognizing and removing this tribe's influence from Europe. Unfortunately Germany lost the war and so Jewish Israel with her attack-dogs America and England are now putting the final Rothschild central banks into place throughout the middle-east making way for the prophesized Zionist Jew World Order government.

What are you working on now? Where do you go from here?
At the moment I am doing everything within my power to spread these truths far and wide. I am making videos, audio books, documentaries, articles, doing radio interviews, writing my sixth book, and even making original rap music covering these topics. *200 Proofs Earth is Not a Spinning Ball* has now been translated into ten foreign languages and several more are in the works. I have created and maintain the International Flat Earth Research Society forum to combat the lies and misinformation of "the Flat Earth Society," which is getting over 50,000 hits per month. They shut down my original forum without warning or reason on New Year Eve 2016, YouTube has blocked and censored several of my videos, Facebook has deleted me thrice and even given my Atlantean Conspiracy group to a team of Freemasons, but regardless of obstacles I vow to continue my mission to expose these truths until the entire world is rightfully educated and throws off these millennial chains of slavery.

Bart Centre

BART CENTRE is an atheist and an author. He came up with
Eternal Earthbound Pets, which was a ridiculously fabulous, as
well as fake, pet-sitting service that hired atheists to care for the
pets of those who have to leave their pets behind because of
the Rapture. The satirical business made news around the world
as many people believed it to be real. He blogs at The Atheist
Camel, and is the author of *The Atheist Camel Chronicles.*

**I loved your website for Eternal Earthbound Pets. I actually sent you
an email at one point to enquire about employment. How many
people did you hear from who knew it was a joke compared to the
those who thought it was real?**

I must have received over 2,000 emails from atheists inquiring about pet
rescuer positions. Naturally, in order to perpetuate the story, I had to decline
but promised that should we ever expand and need additional cadre we'd keep
them in mind. So, don't feel bad you weren't brought on board.

Between atheists, the media, and both sympathetic and irate believers, I
must have received over 4,000 emails during the three years the site was up.
Many were congratulatory on a wonderful concept, others not so much. Some
questioned the sincerity of the service offered, but many more bought into it
than dismissed it. The media certainly bought into it entirely, except for one
reporter who wanted me to sign a paper swearing my site and clients were
real. I declined.

Naturally, I never actually accepted any applications for my post Rapture
pet rescue service, nor received any payment. In fact, the PayPal button
linked to nowhere.

**Did you get a fair amount of press at the time, and if so how did you
handle it? Did you stay in character?**

I launched the site in 2009 soon after my first book, *The Atheist Camel
Chronicles*, was published. My intent was three-fold: to use it as a platform to

"What can be more attractive than the lovely fantasy of living forever in a paradise with your ancestors and your beloved pets?"

promote my book; to conduct a small social experiment to see the reaction of believers; and to basically stick a finger in the eye of fundamentalist born again Rapture believing Christians. It pretty much accomplished all of the above.

Initially it received only incidental publicity. But When the "Reverend" Harold Camping predicted the May 22, 2011, end times and Rapture, well... all hell broke loose. Every major print and broadcast and Internet news outlet was emailing and calling for interviews. I was giving radio and newspaper interviews around the clock ten days or so prior to May 22. I had to keep a schedule to handle the calls that included papers in Russia, South Africa, New Zealand, Canada, Scandinavia, South America, and Australia. New Hampshire's National Public Radio station came to my home to interview me, and the *L.A. Times* send out a photographer to take pictures of myself and my dog for their article. I never broke character. The publicity launched my book into Amazon's top ten best sellers in the atheist genre for about six weeks, alongside Hitchens' and Dawkins' books.

The hardest part of it was having to keep the hoax from my online friends, my readers, and atheist group compatriots. Only one Internet personality knew that this was a hoax.

You describe yourself as an "atheist activist." What does such a person do?

Religion in this nation has a stranglehold on many parts of the country, and has intruded on what the Founding Fathers intended to be a secular government. That's why there is no reference to God, Jesus, Christianity, or any specific religion anywhere in the Constitution.

When religion tries to impose its beliefs and doctrine on others, or wrongfully declare this a "Christian Nation", and seek to truncate the rights of people who do not buy into their doctrine, or uses religion for a justification for war, or prejudice and bigotry, then it is incumbent on thinking people, people of reason, to speak out and take a stand. The days of silently hiding in the closet and allowing "The Church" or any church to run roughshod over people's rights are long gone. So I write letters to the editor of newspapers, I have a blog The Atheist Camel, and of course both my books (my second book, *The Atheist Camel Rants Again!*, was published in 2011)... all are intended to make people aware of, raise their consciousnesses to, the threat that religious fanaticism, in any flavor, can and does have on our nation, and the world as a whole.

I also support and am a dues paying member of a number of Freethinker/ atheist organizations, two of the most important to me being the Freedom From Religion Foundation, and Americans United for the Separation of Church and State. These and other organizations help to expose organized religion's overreach into our laws and rights and where necessary bring legal action on behalf of both believers and non-believers who embrace what Thomas Jefferson referred to as "the wall of separation" between Church and State.

Why do you think so many people believe in such things as God, and the Rapture, and do so without any doubt in their minds as to the truth of their beliefs?

Religion is a holdover from the ancient days where it was used as a societal control and to explain what was unexplainable in a pre-scientific world. It also speaks to man's greatest fear: the fear of death and its finality. What can be more attractive than the lovely fantasy of living forever in a paradise with your ancestors and your beloved pets? It certainly beats the cold hard truth of nothingness and rotting into dust and returning to the basic elements of the universe. Religious people can't accept that realism and finality, so they are happy to accept a fairy tale. And teach it to their children. Happily, in the industrialized world religion is in decline. While the United States remains the most religious industrialized nation, it too has seen dramatic reductions in people professing supernatural/religious belief or adherence to a given religion. In sixty years or so, the number of non-believers in U.S. will be equal to believers, or even be a majority, just like some European countries are today.

What does religion give to this world and what does it take?

The religious will always point toward the charitable functions of their church. And indeed, that does play a role in society. But that same charitable work could be (and is) done without the threat of damnation or the promise of a fantasyland eternal reward; and without the waste of a Catholic Church's vast holdings, gold finery, etc. It doesn't need the mega churches and charlatan televangelists who suck money from the gullible for their personal gain. And there should never be the carrot and stick approach that too many religious charitable organizations use to try and convert victims of tragedy in their greatest hour of need.

On a larger scale, religion helps promote intolerance and ignorance. It was used for centuries to justify racial bigotry, and still often is, and today is the basis for war, justifying misogyny, truncating reproductive rights of women, spreading homophobia, truncating scientific advancement, demonizing education and questioning of the status quo. It works against societal growth and advancement. I often wonder how much more advanced the world would be today had the Church, and much more recently Islamic Wahhabism, had not imposed its fundamentalist mindset, cloistered thought and repression, and killed so many free thinkers and scientists.

To paraphrase and extend Denis Diderot's famous quip: man will never be free until the last king, fascist and tyrant is strangled with the entrails of the last priest, pastor and imam.

Kevin Barrett

KEVIN BARRETT is the author of the book *Questioning the War on Terror* and is the host of the radio show Truth Jihad. He is one of America's best known critics of the so-called war on terror, and considers the Paris and Pulse nightclub shooting, and many others, to be false flags. He formerly was a lecturer at the Univeristy of Wisconsin who specialized in Islamic Culture, because of his views he is no longer teaching classes there, or anywhere else.

You have become well-known for your views on 9-11. Can you sum up what you think happened that day?

9/11 was a coup d'état by the neoconservatives, who are ultra-Zionist, ultra-militarist, ultra-Machiavellian followers of the political philosopher Leo Strauss. The intellectual authors of the crime included such people as Paul Wolfwowitz, who succeeded Paul Nitze as top US strategist; Philip Zelikow, the self-described specialist in "the construction and maintenance of public myths" who wrote the 9/11 Commission Report in chapter outline before the Commission had even convened; and Edward Luttwak, author of the book *Coup d'Etat: A Practical Handbook*, which served for decades as the how-to guide for the planners of what would become September 11th.

All three of those individuals, and about 90% of the other leading neoconservatives, are Zionist-extremist Jews. The overriding strategic objective of 9/11 was—as the 1995 Clean Break document put it—to make sure that "Israel will not only contain its foes; it will transcend them." By "transcending its foes," the authors, including Richard Perle, Douglas Feith, and David Wurmser, meant that Israel would trick the USA and the West into invading or destabilizing those foes. The plan was to "redraw the map of the Middle East" in accordance with the Oded Yinon plan to destroy Israel's unfriendly neighbors by imposing regime change on them, balkanizing them along ethnic and sectarian lines, or otherwise disabling them.

And that is what 9/11 accomplished. The "seven countries in five years" targeted by 9/11 (as explained by General Wesley Clark) were the seven

"They presumably felt that a New Pearl Harbor would unleash US military power and double the military budget overnight, which in fact happened."

leading threats to Israel. As a leading neocon told Clark after 9/11, "We're going to take out seven countries in five years, starting with Iraq, and then Syria, Lebanon, Libya, Somalia, Sudan and, finishing off, Iran."

They destroyed Iraq, with the American occupation allowing Israelis to assassinate most of Iraq's scientific and intellectual leadership while staging false flag bombings to start a Sunni-Shia civil war designed to smash the country into three pieces. They are now destroying Syria in similar fashion. They destabilized Lebanon by assassinating former Prime Minister Rafiq Hariri with an Israeli mini-nuke (the same weapon used in the Bali bombing and perhaps in the demolition of the World Trade Center) while falsely blaming Syria. They destroyed Libya with their al-CIA-duh mercenaries and NATO bombing. They destroyed Somalia by sending their Ethiopian proxies to annihilate the first and last effective government Somalia ever had, the ICU. They destroyed Sudan, splitting off the resource-rich south and handing it to Israel to pillage. And they still yearn to destroy Iran.

For the intellectual authors of the 9/11 coup d'état, the "New Pearl Harbor" they were openly calling for, the destruction of those and other countries—and the massive degradation of the now morally as well as fiscally bankrupt USA—was a small price to pay for enhancing the strategic position of Israel.

Philip Zelikow himself, who probably co-wrote the script for 9/11, gave the game away in a speech at the University of Virginia on September 10, 2002:

"I'll tell you what I think the real threat (is) and actually has been since 1990—it's the threat against Israel. And this is the threat that dare not speak its name, because the Europeans don't care deeply about that threat, I will tell you frankly. And the American government doesn't want to lean too hard on it rhetorically, because it is not a popular sell."

Hating Israel's Muslim enemies, murdering them en masse, and destroying their countries to protect the Zionist occupation of Palestine became a much more "popular sell" after Israel blew up the World Trade Center and falsely blamed it on Arabs and Muslims.

The 9/11 coup was conducted using the standard "drill goes live" scenario that is almost always used in big false flag operations. Webster Tarpley has shown that 9/11 was piggybacked on no less than forty-six drills, war games and terror exercises. More than twenty of these were actually running on the morning of 9/11, the biggest preplanned National Security Special Event Day in history. Two of the exercises running on 9/11 envisioned "planes into buildings" terrorist attack scenarios.

Why did Cheney, Rumsfeld, and other hardliners go along with an Israeli attack on America? The neocon-Zionist coup plotters convinced some hardline US strategists to join their operation, using the pretext that a New Pearl Harbor would allow a "New American Century" of global dominance. The leading neocon think tank, Project for a New American Century (PNAC) issued a document called "Rebuilding America's Defenses" in September 2001. That document openly called for a "New Pearl Harbor," while rewriting the earlier Israel-oriented Clean Break document with a pro-US-empire spin.

The coup plotters created the illusion of hijacked planes crashing into buildings. Though the details are disputed, the simplest way they might have done this would have been to take over actual passenger flights using remote control "hijack termination" systems developed by Rabbi Dov Zakheim's companies. (Zakheim was the Pentagon Conptroller who "lost" 2.3 trillion dollars, seven times the annual military budget, as announced by Rumsfeld on September 10, 2001.) But some evidence points to the possibility of a "plane swap" scenario in which the commercial flights either never took off, or took off and were swapped with military planes; this is the scenario envisioned in the 1962 Operation Northwoods plan for a false flag attack on America, a plan drafted by Gen. Lemnitzer and endorsed by every one of the Joint Chiefs of Staff.

After the "hijacked airliner crashes" into the Twin Towers, the perpetrators blew up the entire World Trade Center—not just the Towers and Building 7, but the other buildings as well. Huge explosions repeatedly rocked all of these buildings, beginning BEFORE the planes hit, as hundreds of witnesses have testified and as videos and photos show. Though 2,500 architects and engineers for 9/11 Truth have risked their reputations and livelihoods to explain the scientific evidence proving that the three skyscrapers were demolished with explosives, anyone with a fifth grade science education and two functioning eyeballs can see that the Towers did not "fall," they exploded. Their explosive "collapses" featured at least ten exclusive characteristics of controlled demolition, including sudden onset, near perfect symmetry, near free-fall acceleration, molten and even evaporated steel in the rubble, pyroclastic dust clouds, high-speed horizontal ejections, and so on. Never in all of history has even one of those characteristics occurred except in controlled demolitions.

World Trade Center Building 7's sudden demise was an even more obvious controlled demolition than the explosive "collapses" of the Twin Towers. A countdown to demolition was even broadcast over police radio. The over-insured alleged-mafiosi WTC landlord Larry Silverstein, who had just bought the Trade Center two months earlier and doubled the terror insurance, confessed on national television to participating in the decision to "pull" (demolish) Building 7.

Silverstein and his Israeli associates controlled World Trade Center security, while the Israeli company ICTS controlled the airports where the allegedly hijacked flights departed. Dr. Alan Sabrosky, the former Director of Studies, Strategic Studies Institute, US Army War College, points out that the Israeli Mossad is the only conceivable candidate for hands-on orchestrator of the coup. But it must be emphasized that the top of the US chain of command, including Bush, Cheney, Rumsfeld, and at least some of the Joint Chiefs, were fully complicit. University of California professor Peter Dale Scott has shown evidence that Cheney and Rumsfeld were part of the planning for 9/11 since their terms in the Ford Administration in the mid-1970s. They presumably felt that a New Pearl Harbor would unleash US military power and double the military budget overnight, which in fact happened. They probably contracted out the details to the Mossad and then just got out of their way.

It should be emphasized that if there is one thing we know with certainty about 9/11, it was that there were no hijackings by human beings (as opposed to remote hijackings, which indeed may have occurred). Not one pilot on any of the four allegedly hijacked planes squawked the hijack code, which would have taken only a few seconds, and would ALWAYS happen in any conceivable hijacking. Additionally, not a single shred of reliable evidence places any of the alleged hijackers, or indeed anyone with Arab or Muslim names, on the planes. There are no official passenger lists. (The unofficial ones released to the media, which are not mutually consistent, feature no Arab names.) There are no ticket stubs or testimony from the airline workers who would have ticketed and boarded any such hijackers. And there is not a single authentic video any of the alleged hijackers at any of the alleged airports from which the alleged attack planes departed.

Given that the perpetrators needed the 100% certainty of successful "plane crashes" at the Trade Towers to provide a cover story for their explosive demolitions, they obviously would not have relied on fallible human hijackers—especially those who, like Hani Hanjour, were incapable of flying a Cessna training aircraft. (And Hanjour, according to the 9/11 Commission, was the "best pilot" among the hijackers!)

The so-called "muscle hijackers" were actually more like five-foot tall 100 pound weaklings. I'm pretty sure I could have taken out any four of them myself, box cutters or no box cutters. The claim that these nineteen low-level CIA-affiliated drug couriers who couldn't even fly Cessnas could pull off the first successful hijacking since the 1970s, much less four of them, and then guide planes into targets at ridiculous, impossible speeds is one of the most ludicrous myths ever entertained by human beings.

The official story is full of elements that are not just absurd, but downright laughable:

Fanatical fundamentalist Muslims who spend most of their time in strip clubs, gambling dens, secure US military facilities, and CIA drug import airstrips disguised as flight schools.

Ultra-hedonistic, ludicrously un-Islamic wannabe suicide hijackers who come to the US a year in advance of their mission and sign up for flying lessons inside the US of all places, then completely flunk out of their flying lessons—yet somehow perform impossible acrobatic stunt feats with 757s.

An alcoholic cocaine-addled "mastermind," Atta, who marches into a Small Business Administration office during the run-up to the attack and aggressively demands a huge sum of cash to buy a crop-duster to drop poison on Washington D,C,, while ranting about his love for Osama Bin Laden.

Magic passports that miraculously appear at "plane crash sites" that otherwise leave no identifiable plane wreckage or bodies.

Magic suitcases that miraculously appear out of nowhere full of incompetently manufactured "incriminating evidence."

The intelligence agents who manufactured the cover story for 9/11 are either the most incompetent covert operators who ever walked the earth, or they are pretending to be so to have a good laugh at what their controlled corporate media can make us believe. This latter "they have a sick sense of humor" hypothesis is explored in SK Bain's The Most Dangerous Book in the World, which readers of this book will surely enjoy.

What of the whole so-called "War on Terror"?
As my book Questioning the War on Terror explains, the whole concept is an Orwellian hoax. Even counting the 3,000 victims of the 9/11 false flag, Americans are far more likely to be hit by lightning or drown in their bathtubs than to die in terrorist attacks.

The "War on Terror" is really a war of terror. Its architects have terrorized us, convincing us to fear a virtually nonexistent threat.

But there is one form of terrorism that is a real threat. It's called war.

To understand why war is terrorism, consider the definition of terrorism: "Attacks on civilians to spread fear for political purposes." This is what wars have always done. During the past two centuries, war has become even more terrorist than in previous ages. Since Sherman marched through Georgia burning, killing and raping civilians, each major war has claimed an increasing percentage of civilian victims. In World War I the "civilian casualty ratio" was 40%. In World War II it was 65%. In many of today's wars it is over 90%. And in World War III it could very well rise to 100%.

Today, over 90% of the victims of "surgical drone strikes" are civilians, many of them women and children. Blowing up entire wedding parties is a favorite pastime of the drone operators.

They also terrorize us with pervasive surveillance. Who among us hasn't ever said or done or written something they would prefer not to see publicized? With their post-9/11 "total information awareness" surveillance state they have colonized our imaginations with the fear that "they" might be spying on us, so we had best not fight back against "them" too hard.

Rich Western populations are controlled by this kind of colonizing of the imagination. Poorer, rebellious populations have their imaginations colonized differently. Instead of having to fear the consequences of surveillance and potential embarrassment, blackmail or prosecution due to that all-pervasive eye-in-the-sky, the people in Afghanistan, Pakistan, Yemen and elsewhere have an even nastier eye-in-the-sky watching them: killer drones that can drop out of nowhere and "bug-splat" their entire families in an instant.

Personally, I am all in favor of having a real all-out war on terrorism. But we need to go after the real terrorists.

In *On Western Terrorism*, Vltchek and Chomsky document fifty-five to sixty million people killed by CIA and US military interventions since World War II. The people responsible for that "American Holocaust," as William Blum calls it, are the real terrorists. They are the ones we should be at war with.

Virtually all terrorism is committed by governments and the corporations who own them. Presidents, generals, CIA directors, and CEOs are responsible for almost all of the terrorism that exists today. They are the ones who need to be either "bug-splatted," or dragged into a Truth and Reconciliation Commission.

Ironically, it is the groups that have declared war on the real terrorists who are labeled "terrorists" by the official propaganda apparatus. FARC has declared war on the murderous Columbian terrorist state (and behind it the US); so the real terrorists in Bogota and Washington put the FARC on their list of "terrorist groups." Likewise with Hamas and Hezbullah and Islamic Jihad, which are pursuing a struggle against not just Israeli state terror, but actual genocide.

Then there are the fake and half-fake (infiltrated) groups like ISIS and al-Qaeda. ISIS is completely synthetic; it is a cartoon series like *Tom and Jerry*, complete with fake beheadings so badly staged and filmed they would have been an embarrassment at a 1970s Alice Cooper concert. ISIS was created by the West to install "a salafist principality in Iraq and Syria" as classified US documents put it. It's a branch of NATO's Operation Gladio B, nothing more.

Al-Qaeda is a "Roger Rabbit" group—it has elements of reality as well as superimposed Hollywood elements of cartoonish fiction. There was a real Osama Bin Laden, but he has been eclipsed by the cartoon villain created by CIA-Mossad Hollywood scriptwriters. And there have been some sincere fighters associated with al-Qaeda, but the infiltrators essentially ran the group and used it to discredit Islamic resistance to empire.

The bottom line is that deception is rampant. Bottom line: We are living in an Orwellian world in which the terrorists call the anti-terrorists "terrorists."

Do you think False Flag Actions are becoming more prevalent? For example what do you think happened at the Boston Marathon?

The Boston Marathon was an obvious false flag attack that was exposed by the alternative media even before the official story was in place and the patsies named. The proof is available to anyone with eyes. The exploded backpacks (photos courtesy of the FBI) were not on the backs of the Tsarnaev brothers. Those backpacks were carried, and the bombs set off, by two Craft International mercenaries.

And Sandy Hook? What did you feel about that?
The preponderance of the evidence I've seen suggests that it, too, was probably a false flag hoax. The multiple lines of argument making that case are developed in the book, *Nobody Died at Sandy Hook*, which has been banned by Amazon.

Though I'm not 100% certain what really happened at Sandy Hook, I am outraged that Florida Atlantic University professor James Tracy was fired for asking good questions about this highly suspicious event. Professor Tracy was tenured, which should have protected his right to pursue controversial lines of inquiry. That is the whole point of the tenure system! Yet rather than refute his arguments—which would have been a simple "slam dunk" if the official story is correct—his detractors chose to use deceptions, distortions, and outright lies to get him fired from his job.

The same thing happened to me at the University of Wisconsin (except that I was untenured, which made me an easier target). Politicians who didn't like my research on 9/11 attacked me not because of anything I did on the job, but because they didn't like the views I expressed on a radio show. Likewise, Professor Tracy was fired not because of anything he said in the classroom or wrote in academic journals, but due to views he expressed on his blog.

If State Rep. Steve Nass, and behind him Lynn Cheney and Karl Rove, didn't like my views of 9/11, they should have found someone to refute them. Yet when the Debate Club at the University of Wisconsin tried to arrange a debate, not a single professor was willing to defend the Official Conspiracy Theory against me. Wisconsin newspapers editorialized, begging the university to find at least one professor who could debate me and show why my arguments are wrong. But none stepped forward. A few years later, my backers offered $1,000 to any teacher (professor, lecturer or teacher's assistant) who would debate me on 9/11. No response. The offer was raised to $2,000. Still no response. The offer still stands today.

Likewise, Florida Atlantic University (and whoever was pressuring them) should have been able to find someone to argue convincingly against James Tracy's views. Instead, they summarily fired him. Obviously Professor Tracy's views must be difficult to refute.

I know there have been some issues around you teaching classes on Islamic history and culture because of your views. How has speaking what you feel to be the truth affected your life and your career?

I am no longer employable in the American academy. The political witch-hunt led by the Wisconsin Republican Party succeeded in that respect. The University of Wisconsin Engineering School lost more than half a million dollars in canceled donations within twenty-four hours after I appeared on the *Hannity Show* on Fox News in July 2006. I'm sure there were other financial hits as well. Any American university that hired me would expose itself to political attacks and likely take a financial beating.

Then Dean of Humanities Howard Ross has testified that I was turned down for a tenure-track Islam and Humanities job at the University of Wisconsin-Whitewater purely due to my research on 9/11. He said I was the best candidate of the three finalists, then the only candidate after the other two went elsewhere; but the hiring committee was told that I could not be hired due to the 9/11 issue, so the university returned a huge grant to the federal government and did not fill the position.

The same thing happened with another Islam and Humanities job at the University of Illinois for which I applied. The university refused to fill the position and returned federal grant money, claiming there were no qualified candidates. In fact, I was highly qualified; how many Ph.D. Arabic and Islamic Studies scholars are there who have taught college humanities and hold four advanced degrees in various world literatures?

So my career as a university instructor is over. But my work in education continues. I am making a much more important contribution to public education as an independent author, editor, journalist, pundit and talk radio host than I ever could have as a professor.

More importantly, I am benefiting spiritually and psychologically by following the "path of blame" (for speaking the truth) which is the path trodden by all the prophets. I am certainly not saying I'm a prophet. But, as Woody Allen says about God, we need role models. OBVIOUSLY we are all supposed to emulate the prophets. A Christian who doesn't make the utmost effort to act like Jesus isn't much of a Christian.

Telling a very important truth, and being reviled for it by the "ungrateful truth-concealers" (kuffar, sometimes mistranslated as "infidels") is the greatest thing anybody could possibly be doing. So with amazement and gratitude I give thanks to God for this miraculous opportunity to make the most of my time on Earth.

"...they don't even realize their obedience has been achieved by means that have completely circumvented their consciousness"

Mark Diehl

MARK DIEHL is an author and a political activist. His latest
book is *Seventeen*. According to his website, Army of the
Doomed, he believes that obedience and conformity are
becoming humanity's most important survival skills, and that
we are thus evolving into a corporate species. He has been
homeless in Japan, and a corporate lawyer in Chicago.

How did you go from corporate lawyer to indie author?
I never wanted to be an author. It seemed a terribly immature goal
to have. I wanted to do something stable and profitable. In spite of
myself, though, I was writing before I was a lawyer.

As a young adult, I lived and worked in the local economies of five countries.
Like other explorers, I got to experience and compare the ways human cultures
differed, but I also began to wonder about the reasons they developed as they
did. I became fascinated with the idea that culture is inseparable from factors
like population density and resource availability, and I was never able to stop
thinking about it.

In Japan, I was shocked to see how oppressive and controlling the school
system was to the children. Jetlagged and walking around early in the morning
there, you can sometimes see the kids all lined up outside, bowing in unison
to their teacher before starting their exercises. The whole educational process
seems designed to strip them completely of their individuality and turn them
into fungible worker robots. In cramped little grocery stores they sold square
watermelons that had been grown in plastic boxes so that they could be stacked
on shelves, and I realized the same thing was happening to the children. In
other countries with more space and resources available, watermelons and kids
can grow up without such rigidity, but of course the entire world is now running
out of space and resources.

I'd get ideas about something at the interface of culture, politics, history,
and other population dynamics, and find myself unable to work or sleep until
I figured it out on paper. Taking copious notes this way over many years, I

eventually worked them into a comprehensive model for predicting where humanity would develop from this point.

I was working in South Korea when my Korean girlfriend's powerful family found out she was dating me. They beat her and locked her in a room, telling her they were going to arrange a marriage to the first Korean they could find, but she escaped and came to my place at four in the morning, covered in bruises. In the interest of protecting the family name from scandal, they used their connections to try and apprehend her, and ended up chasing us out of the country with the police. We fled to Hong Kong and got married, but visa issues stranded us there for several weeks with no income. By the time we made it to the United States we had less than one dollar in cash between us, and we owed credit cards for the plane tickets. We settled into a single room behind a convenience store in Iowa City, Iowa, taking menial jobs.

Through it all, I kept writing in my notebooks, distilling what I'd learned into new versions. Humanity's future got clearer to me all the time, though back then it was still mostly just a hazy outline. I felt utterly compelled to do it, but angry with myself for succumbing to such a pointless waste of precious time and energy when I should have been working harder to dig us out of the financial hole we were in.

Attending graduate school would let us get student loans and move into subsidized student housing. My wife went to a master's program for information science, and I truly didn't care what I did as long as it was a real, grown up job (i.e. not writing). I applied to three schools at the University of Iowa that I thought I might be able to tolerate, at the Colleges of Law, Dentistry, and Business Administration. Each school was a backup for the others, in case they rejected me. After I was accepted to all three programs, I decided that I would be the first person to get degrees from all of them.

The dental school refused to accommodate the other schedules, so I dropped it. I hadn't ever been interested in the profession so much, anyway. I was good at science and I thought it'd be a safe way to a paycheck, but picking at teeth never sounded like much of a life.

The MBA program had an orientation where we had to learn to work together by building towers out of note cards. The materials showed the program would involve a whole lot of pointless projects like that. I left at noon and never returned.

I attended law school and ended up with a doctorate, along with staggering debt. The only way to pay it back was to work in a law firm, so I did. I got a job in a high-volume litigation practice where I became known as being good in the courtroom, and eventually was brought up to the big leagues as a litigator at a giant multinational firm. I sued huge corporations on behalf of other huge corporations. While there, I noticed that the enforced culture inside those institutions resembled what I had seen in Asia.

The ideas grew until something quite disturbing became clear to me. I'm now convinced that humanity, as we know it, will soon disappear from this planet. This is not because we'll wipe ourselves out in some catastrophe, but because we are becoming something else. Generation by generation, we reward those who can exist inside giant organizations and punish those who can't. The most corporate are better able to provide for the next generation, who are more likely to grow into their parents' roles in society. We are evolving into a corporate species.

When the technology became available, I started blogging. I wrote about how Japan's conformist culture allowed it to develop the world's highest population density, on a few rocks out in the ocean with no resources. I looked at how ants and bees had once been more individualistic, like modern beetles are today, and slowly evolved into what biologists call super organisms, where the colony or hive is all that matters and individuals are routinely sacrificed. I warned my readers that because corporations and other enormous organizations had so much power, they were claiming all the world's resources for themselves. A few people listened, but the material was too dry and too complex to reach the masses. If I was going to get this idea across, it would have to be through fiction.

I left the multinational firm and attended another graduate school, this time in fiction writing at the University of Chicago. I worked and practiced until I was able to write interesting and engaging fiction, and started on my *Seventeen* trilogy, which traces humanity's evolution from today's corporate control to tomorrow's super organism. *Volume One: The Book of Eadie* won an award. Now I'm finishing up *Volume Two: The Book of Wanda*. I hope it will be as warmly received.

I still don't actually want to be an author, but this trilogy won't let me rest. My *Seventeen* trilogy features a story I made up and characters I created, but the world those characters inhabit is truly the future of humanity. I started it in the hope that people would see where we're headed and stop it, but now I see that it's inevitable.

You describe yourself as a post-objectivist fiction writer. Can you break down what that means?

I'm talking here as a genre of fiction, not necessarily a philosophy. I'm much more interested in seeing what will happen than in deciding what ought to happen. The bottom line is that corporations will not save us, and in fact, will develop into the most oppressive structures yet known to mankind. The soulless and immortal corporation is probably the most dangerous of all human inventions, and is currently eclipsing the previously most dangerous form of organization, the nation-state. (The nation-state replaced the kingdom in the same way, as did the kingdom to the tribes it replaced.)

All institutions dehumanize us. There's a simple trade we make whenever we decide (or are forced) to subject ourselves to the authority of any organization: We give up our autonomy to gain the group's protection. This is true with all human groups, from street gangs and cults to national governments and the corporations that dwarf and control them. Our institutions get larger and more powerful all the time, and the level of surrender they demand from their subjects is becoming proportionally deeper.

Because societies grant governments a monopoly on violence, it's tempting to imagine government as our only oppressor. I wish I could be one of those people who fantasize that simply getting rid of government would fix everything. In fact, democratically elected governments are among the more benign forms of human control. What's really stripping us of our freedom and individual autonomy are the institutions working just out of our field of vision, slowly accumulating power through control of information and resources, not subject to voting or recall. Through selection of political candidates with funding, these forces have now infiltrated formerly democratically elected governments around the world.

Some of these organizations are multinational corporations, but there are other formats as well. Take lobbying by the American Medical Association, for example, which has successfully gained for doctors such legal control over our bodies that taking medicine without written permission from them is now a crime. People always organize to concentrate power, and once they've done so, they use the new power to build their organizations and concentrate more power. If we were to strip power from government, a vacuum will form that religions, corporations, mafias and other groups will expand to fill.

Reason is mankind's strongest superpower, but unfortunately it is easily supplanted from outside. People surrender their own rationality quite easily, becoming instruments of someone else's agenda. That concentrates power in a group, which puts us right back to the cycle of increased growth and further concentration of power. Meanwhile, what we think of as government is already being hollowed out and replaced with corporate agendas, at all levels from Washington, D.C., to the local city council. If you get rid of government, corporations will just have private enforcers do what they've been making cops and bureaucrats do to you lately. Either way, you end up with power still being concentrated into groups that are ever more powerful and controlling.

As bad as the political climate is now, where do you see it going?
Remember when companies used to lure in the best candidates with juicy benefits packages that provided health care, retirement, and all kinds of other great stuff like vacations and bonuses? Then, slowly, they kind of dried up again, right after all those people had become specialized in a narrowly defined job with limited mobility, and after most of the competition had been put out of business. Still, those corporate packages were better than what anyone else got.

The new corporate perk will be security. America is slowly starving atop mountains of guns, and the climate gets tenser and more desperate everyday. Meanwhile, Americans who are being taxed to death to fund corporate subsidies and wars for corporate profit will clamor for "smaller government." They'll receive it in the time-honored tradition of reduced services, including police. Fewer services mean more desperation and more danger.

Corporate people will live in "safe" company housing and be escorted to work by private security forces in armored vehicles, much like today's prisoners. Soon every corporation will have an armed security division. In response to the arrival of this corporate feudalism, the national governments of the world (which will probably all have been absorbed into the United States at this point, at least de facto if not officially) will arm their own soldiers with outrageous weapons. Various corporations will vie for control of the government but find its bureaucracy resistant to direct control because government will always exist primarily for its own purposes.

That's the future: Corporate armies will struggle for power amid federal authorities that serve in some capacity between private enforcers and corporate clergy. Only those individuals who are of the most value to multinational corporations will be rewarded with healthy food, medicine, education, and security. Over time the corporate workers will become a tiny ruling class, but only through their service as slaves.

This is the world where I've set my *Seventeen* trilogy.

You have said that you are fascinated by power dynamics. How does one become powerful, and how does one become weak?
Have you seen these organizations asking you to donate money so they can buy a goat or a chicken for someone in a primitive farming village? I've always been fascinated by those, especially since the ones I saw tended to phrase their requests in vaguely religious terms.

I imagine the strangers coming into town for the first time, maybe just with a few chickens. They make an offer to the impoverished locals: Anyone who sits through a sermon can take home an egg. They give the sermon and everyone who is still there gets his or her egg, everyday for maybe a week. People bring their children, and the kids get eggs, too. They bring their families, their neighbors, and their friends. Everyone gets eggs. At the end of the week, those who sat through all the sermons are seven eggs stronger and seven eggs healthier than the ones who chose not to attend. The egg-fed kids start winning at whatever sports people play in such places, presumably involving sticks and mud or whatever.

Now, notice that how you feel about this story so far depends on your interpretation of my word, "sermon." If you imagine these people spreading a kind version of what you consider a true religion, you'll feel differently about the scenario than if you imagine one of those child-raping cults that often make their way to Third World countries. What's important to remember is that from the perspective of the villagers, the deal is the same: Sit through the sermon and get an egg. White hats or black, the rodeo proceeds in the same way.

Next the strangers ask for volunteers to help with the sermons, especially targeting the people who brought in more friends and family already. At the end of another week, each of the volunteers gets to take a chicken home. Everyone in the new congregation sees that the volunteers now have their own personal chickens and have achieved a new level of wealth and prestige. The people who rejected the sermons are now dozens of eggs weaker, and they find themselves competing in a new economy where some of their neighbors now have eggs to trade. In terms of power, prestige, health, and economics at the village level, these independent folks are now way behind.

And so it goes. The sermons continue, and the lessons compound. Whatever's being preached, the people are learning that their compliance provides a real world benefit. The ones who win are those who "give back" to the group, and they form a new inner circle. Eventually some of these people are even given a goat. They go out in the community and trade their eggs and goat milk for other things, building their own wealth through transactions with their neighbors. Soon the most zealous believers are also the richest and most powerful members of the community.

Again, we don't know what the strangers are after. One thing that's clear, though, is that they've just cultivated a power structure in the village, with themselves as the ultimate source of wealth, values, and authority.

Few of us in developed nations have, or even want to have, our own chickens. Don't be fooled. In Third World countries, owning more chickens means having more power. In our world, we're the chickens. The more people you control, and the more work and devotion you're able to squeeze out of those people, the higher the reward you'll receive from those who are squeezing you. That reward, whether given in dollars, chickens, or promotions, is actually always the same. At its core, it is power over other people.

How do we change what is happening now? Can we?

The evolution of humanity from a species of individuals into a species of super organisms is inevitable. The question is not whether it will happen, for it is happening all around us everyday. Rather, we should concern ourselves with how long individuals might be able to coexist among superorganistic human organizations. My research and experience says that we individuals will not live alongside hyperorganized humanity, and in fact, that independent individuals are being squeezed out of the human gene pool at an alarming rate, through means as varied as denial of medical care, starvation, homelessness, and suicide.

This is not a new phenomenon. Imagine being a farmer a few thousand years ago. When a lone bandit comes and tries to take your crops, you and your family can fight him off. When a gang of thugs comes, your village can band together and handle it. Then one day you look up and you see an entire Roman legion. No matter what level of organization you've achieved, they will wipe you out. Once militaristic hierarchies evolved, every army in the world quickly became an efficient, top-down hierarchy or was wiped out by one that was. In modern times, we accept as normal that there are armies the size nations once were. Today's typical example of any organization, from a government to a church to a corporation, is gigantic compared to its predecessors.

I believe corporations will be the organizational model that replaces individual humanity, rather than the more archaic forms of organization like religions or governments based on geography. The older forms took in whoever came along or was born into them, because in the earlier days sheer numbers of people gave an organization power. Now corporations can select only those individuals that prove and ability to provide them a benefit, and eject the rest in the same way a biological organism can slough off cells. As an organism develops, there are programmed cell deaths that occur to allow it to morph into a mature form, in a process called apoptosis. In our case, corporate structures develop by casting out people.

It's often said that society is three meals from anarchy. People will put up with a lot when their stomachs are full that would enrage them if they were hungry. We imagine we're not as close to the edge as we really are, because the food supply has been tweaked and manipulated. We hear that modern processed foods are unhealthy because they contain too much fat, salt, cholesterol, and so on, but this isn't the whole story. Actually, processed foods are dangerous mostly because those bad things are all they offer. Yes, we get fatter and our arteries clog, but we still starve for all the nutrients we're supposed to get from food. In terms of actual nutrition, we are billions of meals past the three missed ones that were supposed to topple society, but we don't notice because we're stuffed with garbage.

Our society does the same with information that it does with food. Like a little kid who refuses all but the most processed of foods, the average follower of today will only accept information about leaders a sound bite at a time, each one prepared by professional psychologists and spin doctors to ensure maximum compliance. What's terrifying about this is that they don't even realize their obedience has been achieved by means that have completely circumvented their consciousness. Just as they don't know they're starving, they also don't know they've stopped thinking.

"...those of privilege in the U.S. are starting to get a taste for what much of the rest of the world has been feeling for an awfully long time."

Mimi Soltysik

MIMI SOLTYSIK was the Socialist Party USA candidate for President in the 2016 Elections. I once tried to join the Socialist party, and couldn't find anyone that would get back to me about it. If Mimi becomes President, I am sure that will change. According to campaign literature, the Socialist Party USA stands for "the abolition of every form of domination and exploitation, whether based on social class, gender, race/ethnicity, age, education, sexual orientation, or other characteristics."

You are running for President for the Socialist Party, USA. How is that whole scene going so far?

It's been a blast. It was hard to anticipate how things might turn out when we first started this. The messaging we're sending with the campaign is a bit different from what folks might normally expect from a campaign, particularly with regard to the need to shift the focus away from D.C. politics and toward community organizing. Our hope was that, once using the media opportunities that we might receive, folks would respond with interest, and as a result, we'd be able to open a dialog about socialism and how to achieve it.

How do you think the word "Socialist" became such a scary word to so many people in America?

The Cold War might be the obvious answer. So much false propaganda, and, at the time, it was much more difficult to quickly call the state's bluff.

So many people are poor, and have nothing, but are still staunch capitalists. This confuses the hell out of me. Do you have an answer for this?

Some of this is the result of the answer to your prior question. Capitalism is devious as hell. Marx talked about how the capitalist class divides the working class in order to maintain power.

How long can this current system collapse before it crumbles?

I think it is crumbling. The effects of climate change are here, and it's only going to get worse. Income inequality continues to grow. The state continues to slaughter our oppressed communities at home, and U.S. imperialism has murdered millions and will continue to murder millions more barring a revolutionary shift.

Perhaps, to a small degree, those of privilege in the U.S. are starting to get a taste for what much of the rest of the world has been feeling for an awfully long time. I'm not saying that I enjoy seeing our privileged communities suffer. But I think it's important to be realistic about how that privilege was established.

What can people do, other than violent uprising, to change what is going on?

I think that working within our communities is critical. Opening ourselves up to the idea of community. Listening. Developing networks. Identifying pressure points within the system and organizing around strategies designed to attack those pressure points. I know that this all sounds like an abstraction or incredibly superficial, but honestly, I see little hope for any sort of revolutionary change without communities throughout the country—connected even loosely— prepared to plan and act.

Caitlin Darcy

I know CAITLIN DARCY, and I knew she was a dominatrix in high school. This made me curious. She was kind enough to answer some questions about how that whole thing went down. Caitlin Darcy is a pseudonym. In real life she is a journalist who lives in Los Angeles.

It kind of sounds like a bad afterschool movie, but how did being a teenage dominatrix come about?

It went like this: I was in high school, and had just gotten laid off from my job—I was doing data entry at a worker's comp law firm in Hollywood like two or three days a week. And even though I hated the fuck out of the job (I was a secretary's bitch), it sent me into this weird depression.

I grew up super poor, which is not the typical narrative for a Jew growing up in LA, and I really needed money to eat lunch and go to the movies and stuff. My friends were all really rich, and this compounded the anxiety.

Anywho, I kept bitching and moaning about how I was jobless and depressed to my boyfriend at the time. So he went onto Craigslist and found a job listing that said they needed someone for a non-sex, non-nude role in a BDSM film—for one day. It didn't sound like a terrible way to make money. I replied and, to my surprise at the time, heard back and set up an interview.

I walked more than a mile from my high school to a gas station to meet a woman with a husky voice named Cassandra (we'd spoken on the phone). I was kind of wild in that way—I'd just meet someone at a gas station that I knew nothing about, looking like a little deranged schoolgirl. I pictured Cassandra as some statuesque red head, but she actually was (and is!) a tiny Asian woman.

It started becoming clear to me that there really was no film—that what Cassandra really wanted me to do was work "sessions" with submissive men for $200 an hour. Sessions are basically one-hour "scenes" (for those familiar with BDSM terms). Mind you, I was eighteen at the time and had absolutely no experience with the wild world of fetish and sex work.

I kept telling Cassandra I couldn't do it; I didn't think I had it in me. But I have been kinky since as long as I can remember, and it turned out I was kind of a

"Sometimes it can be hard to face someone at breakfast after they've done horrible things to your bum hole."

natural. Surprisingly, my boyfriend totally supported me when I started working and would drive me to most of my sessions because I didn't have a car. He'd also fix computers and tech stuff around the dungeon, and Cassandra loved him. The money was intoxicating: Suddenly I had wads of hundreds stuffed into a notebook and could afford to buy clothes and concert tickets. But I saved most of it, and the money basically supported me through college.

And—believe it or not—Cassandra and I are still really good friends to this day, even though I have retired as a pro Dom.

Being paid to be in control, how much of it was a turn on and how much of it was just plain old nasty?
You know, I surprised myself by getting off on things that I would have never fantasized about independently. It made me realize that fantasies are not set in stone. If I had chemistry with a particular person, and they really wanted to please me (and I don't mean with their penis) and were sensitive to my needs, then we could both enjoy ourselves. For example, I had a client that is a pretty well-known actor, and he was into extreme humiliation and face sitting. For some reason, even though I would have never ever pursued what we did in sessions in my personal life, I always got off during our sessions.

Of course there was some nasty stuff. There are some freakity freaks out there! When you're doing stuff like fucking someone in the ass with a strap on, things can get pretty literally dirty. Some of these guys were old, ugly, stinky—all the things guys can be. And because you're being paid for your services and have to be "on demand," you're definitely not always going to be in the mood to kick someone's ass or whatever.

But being in control specifically, that was a turn on. Having guys call me "goddess" and worship my feet—I couldn't help but internalize some of the praise. A few months in, my confidence was blazing. Random guys at bars would come up to me and start confessing their submissive fantasies within seconds. That's how much power I had at my peak.

Did you have many regulars? What were their scenes?
I did have quite a few regulars. I am not a naturally stern or mean person, so I attracted people who like sensual domination. My specialty was humiliation and verbal domination. I was like a nerdy, bratty Lolita-type.

What were your limits? What would you not do?
So... for some reason I was born with a high tolerance for weird shit. It takes A LOT to shock me.

But one thing I could not and would not do is a Roman Shower, which is vomiting on someone. (1) I can't make myself throw up, and (2) I find the smell and look of vomit intolerable. There was one girl I worked with who was bulimic and was a pro at Roman Showers, and it horrified me when I watched. Also, I did not have sex with clients. Some people conflate pro Dom work with prostitution, but it's not the same at all.

You have left that life behind you in a professional capacity, but do you still indulge in dominance?
From time to time, though it seems like less and less as the distance between me and my last session grows. Submissive men are still attracted to me—I must be marked or something—and a hot sub boy can bring out, uh, tendencies in me. But being a Dom is a lot of work! If I assume the dominant role in the bedroom or otherwise, I have to love that person enough to want to possess them—or they have to be serving me in a way that's worth my while.

I've been with the same guy for more than three years now. When we first started hooking up/dating, he was very submissive to me. But as time went on and our relationship became more domestic, we mellowed out on a lot of the kink.

I think a big reason why men seek out and pay pro Doms instead of finding a girlfriend to play with is that it's a lot easier to compartmentalize kink than integrate it into your workaday relationship. Sometimes it can be hard to face someone at breakfast after they've done horrible things to your bum hole.

Keith Preston

KEITH PRESTON is the main man behind the website Attack the System, whose motto is "Pan-anarchism against the state, Pan-Secessionism against the empire" and which is maintained by American Revolutionary Vanguard, a dissident tendency within the international anarchist movement based in North America. He is the author of *Attack the System: A New Anarchist Perspective for the 21st Century.* He thinks things should be different.

Can you tell me a little bit about the American Revolutionary Vanguard and what it stands for?

American Revolutionary Vanguard was founded in the late 1990s by a coalition of anarchists in the North American anarchist movement who wished to pursue a different direction from what was the norm among anarchists in North America at the time. The rest of the anarchist movement was usually oriented towards promoting one of three perspectives: countercultural lifestyle concerns (ranging from veganism to alternative sexuality to squatting to punk music and bicycling), or a kind of clichéd ultra-leftism of the kind that had been developed by Marxist-Leninist and Maoist tendencies within the New Left (such as an emphasis on "white skin privilege" and radical feminism), or old-guard anarcho-syndicalism that had been influenced by early twentieth-century syndicalist tendencies such as the Industrial Workers of the World.

We wished to pursue an entirely new direction which would be oriented towards uniting all forms of anarchist, decentralist, libertarian, anti-state, and anti-authoritarian thought around the common purpose of abolishing the state and decentralizing power towards the level of the natural community, and forging a society-wide consensus for this purpose. Much of what we did at the time was a bit tongue in cheek as well. For example, our original name, American Revolutionary Vanguard, doesn't really mean anything. The word "vanguard" is something of a taboo in anarchist circles because of its association with the Marxist-Leninist idea of the "vanguard party." So we always claimed we were trying to reclaim the good name of the word "vanguard." Ironically, back

"Anarchism is a philosophy that advocates for the abolition of the state, not a prescription for how one should live within the context of a state-saturated society."

then many in the anarchist milieu were suspicious of us and thought we were communists, but now we're more likely to be mislabeled as fascists. But the original purpose of American Revolutionary Vanguard was the same as it is now: the formation of an anti-state front.

Can you explain a bit about pan-secessionism and what it means to your philosophy?

Pan-secessionism is a tactical concept that involves the actual application of our philosophy to real world political events. Simply put, our goal is for smaller political and economic units to secede from larger ones. State and provinces would secede from national governments, and cities and communities would secede from states and provinces, all the way down to the neighborhood level. "Power to the neighborhoods" is a common slogan we like to use towards this purpose. Presumably, there could be a parallel economic secession where local and regional branches of industries and managerial units secede and begin to practice autonomy and self-management as well. The concept of pan-secessionism has its roots in two basic ideas. One is the idea of political secession in the form of regional or local autonomist movements such as those currently found in Scotland, the Basque and Catalan regions of Spain, in multiple regions of the US, in Palestine, Tibet, Chechnya and many other places. In the United States, this is a particularly relevant concept given that the United States was essentially founded as a secession of the original thirteen colonies from the British monarchy.

The other idea which has influenced the concept of pan-secession is the old anarchist idea of the "general strike." The notion behind the general strike is that workers establish control over production by means of a mass strike that turns into a popular revolution. The old anarcho-syndicalist labor organizations used to advocate for this idea in the era of classical anarchism. However, the concept of pan-secessionism takes this idea much further and advocates a general strike not just in the industrial sectors, but a popular strike against the state and its institutions altogether in the form of regional and local secession, a labor strike, a tax strike, a tenants' strike, a students' strike, and a military strike, in such a way that ruling class institutions are completely undermined.

In certain parts of our population it is cool to say that one is an anarchist. I know some people that call themselves "anarchists" but yet pay their taxes, follow established laws, and generally do what the government tells them to do. Is it possible to be an anarchist and also follow the established rules of one's government?

Anarchism is a philosophy that advocates for the abolition of the state, not a prescription for how one should live within the context of a state-saturated society. Some anarchists choose the route of becoming what have been called "illegalists" and act in open defiance of the state and its laws and commands. Others prefer to live within the system and work for more piecemeal reforms, or simply try to obtain the maximum degree of individual or collective self-sufficiency possible given the circumstances. No one way is the correct way. Instead, it is best for there to be different kinds of anarchists working to undermine the state in many different ways. There are many different ways in which anarchists go about fighting the state. At present, some anarchists in the Kurdish region have formed militias that are involved in direct-armed resistance to ISIS and have formed a quasi-anarchist community in Rojava. Other types of anarchists have formed intentional nations like Liberland, and others are working through unconventional political parties like the Pirate Party, and still others are engaged in direction action around such concerns as environmental preservation. The best approach for anarchists to take towards these questions would be to let a thousand flowers bloom.

It is obvious to most thinking people that our current system is way too wrong to last, but still the vast majority of people do not take anarchy seriously. What are today's anarchists doing wrong? What needs to happen to change that? Is there a place for violence?
Most people are not anarchists because anarchists have not yet succeed at the task of educating others about anarchism to the degree necessary for a popular consensus in favor of anarchism to develop. Our goal should be to grow all forms of resistance until these collectively become a political majority, and then a super-majority, along with the overarching strategic concept of pan-secession and other related ideas. But this is something that takes a great deal of time, and patience is very much in order. The idea that the emperor is to be worshiped as a sun-god did not disappear overnight, nor did the idea of divine right of kings. The false abstractions that are used to justify modern states will not disappear immediately either. However, we as anarchists should be working to undermine and destroy the false pieties that are used to uphold modern states such as the idea of the social contract, the idea that the state is somehow a protector of natural rights or human rights, the idea that the state is somehow based or could ever be based on the idea of popular sovereignty or some kind of mythical general will, and the idea that a mere 51% vote legitimizes whatever a particular state wishes to do.

The purpose of the state is to monopolize territory, control resources, exploit subjects, protect an artificially privileged ruling class, and expand its own power. Other claims on behalf of the state are merely evasion and obfuscation. It might be said that the state is merely a mafia with a flag, and a far more insidious institution than the mafia given the much greater level of destructiveness and deceptiveness. Our ambition as anarchists should be to develop a social consensus towards the viewpoint that the state is no more legitimate than slavery or the divine right of kings and other such ills that existed in the past.

As for what today's anarchists are doing wrong, many anarchists have put the proverbial cart before the horse, in the sense that their primary focus is on many of things that we decided were a distraction from the building of a social consensus towards anarchism when we started American Revolutionary Vanguard nearly twenty years ago. Many anarchists have allowed themselves to become absorbed by so-called "progressivism" and consequently are no more effective at challenging the legitimacy of the state than ordinary political tendencies that accept the state as a matter of principle or presumption. Many anarchists are merely activists around popular social issues, or promoting countercultural lifestyles, and consequently have lost sight of the wider picture that involves the need to forge a consensus towards the abolition of the state.

An excess of sectarianism also exists among anarchists. The anarchist movement is largely divided into multiple hyphenated tendencies such as anarcho-communism, anarcho-syndicalism, anarcha-feminism, anarcho-primitivism, anarcho-collectivism, anarcho-capitalism, egoist anarchism, and many, many other tendencies. It would be preferable for anarchists to attempt to find ways to move past these sectarian ideas and find common principles around which anarchists can unite, and common issues through which anarchists can broaden their appeal to larger numbers of people. As for the question of violence, that is a subject on which anarchists do not agree and have never agreed. In the past, there have been anarchists who used terrorist methods to advance their ideals, and other anarchists who are pacifists. I lean towards the idea that different kinds of tactics are appropriate or necessary in different kinds of circumstances.

Another word, other than anarchy, that gets thrown around without people knowing what it means is "fascist."

I have read a few articles that claimed your pan-secessionism tends towards fascism and white nationalism; can you shed any light on that?
Fascism is a concept that has absolutely nothing to do with either anarchism as a political theory, or pan-secessionism as an anarchist tactic. Fascism is an idea which proclaims "All within the state, nothing outside the state, nothing against the state" which is how fascism was described by its founder, Benito Mussolini. Clearly, this is the polar opposite idea of anarchism which seeks to abolish the state. Fascism and Nazism are totalitarian ideologies of the Right just as Marxism-Leninism, Stalinism, Maoism, Pol Potism and Kim's Juche Idea are totalitarian ideologies of the Left. But anarchism stands resolutely

opposed not only to totalitarian manifestations of the state but to the state in any of its manifestations.

The concept of nationalism is also viewed with suspicion by anarchists because historically nationalism has been used to justify statist oppression, imperialism and interstate warfare, and nationalism continues to be used for these purposes in some instances. However, there are also people who call themselves anarcho-nationalists, tribal-anarchists or national-anarchists who will affirm the legitimacy of nations, regions, and communities based on a shared culture, language, ethnicity, heritage or religion while denying the legitimacy of the state or the exploitation and cooptation of these things by the state. An example is the way in which the Native American and First Nations tribes, the Australian aboriginals, the Kurds, Tibetans, and many other identifiable population groups are nations but not a state. An even bigger controversy among anarchists involves the idea of whether European or Caucasian ethnic groups can have legitimate claims to identities of these kinds given the past legacy of the European states in perpetrating colonialism, imperialism, the slave trade, ethnic cleansing of indigenous people, apartheid, world wars, and the Holocaust.

While there is strong disagreement among anarchists on this question, I hold to the view that anarchism should recognize the principles of self-determination for all, including all ethnic groups, cultures, religions, nationalities, regions, and communities, and for people of all races, ethnicities, genders, sexual orientations, and lifestyles. There are also anarchist tendencies representing black or African-American anarchists, Zapatista anarchists, native or indigenous anarchists, Buddhist anarchists, Christian anarchists, pagan anarchists, and Islamic anarchists. For this reason, anarchists should give those anarchists that identify with some kind of European ethnicity, culture or religion their seat at the table as well. This is the perspective that I believe is most compatible with the ideals of anarchism as a movement that stands in opposition to statism, capitalism, imperialism, aggressive war, and authoritarianism, and which upholds individual liberty, decentralism, voluntarism, federalism, mutual aid, cooperativism, syndicalism, communitarianism, pluralism, human scale institutions, intellectual freedom, free inquiry, free speech, and freedom of association.

Jani Leinonen

JANI LEINONEN is an artist an activist and a socialist. He is perhaps best known for his satirical *Tony is Back!* commercial series which feature Kellog's cereal mascot Tony the Tiger, dealing with prostitution, police brutality and suicide bombers. and for being arrested for stealing and beheading a statue of Ronald McDonald as a member of the group The Food Liberation Army.

Your website says you are "tired of a world where real alternatives are impossible to imagine" Why do you think that people don't seem to understand that things could actually be different?
Our imagination might be paralyzed by the economical and political system. If there was anything good about the Cold War it was the counterforce of alternative systems that forced us to think about the function of the system. Now we live historically in the most totally capitalist world and even the thoughts of alternative models of society have been exhausted. But fundamentally it is about what kind of story we are being told about what we as humans are. Now the only storyline is that we are competitive, as a race and as individuals— even though the science actually contradicts this, because we have much more biological reward systems that reward collaboration over competition.

Can you tell me a bit about the McDonald's incident, and your subsequent arrest?
The kidnapping of Ronald exceeded all my aims big time. Although I did shed some tears in jail in the end it was very good for the project. The whole idea to the kidnapping came from a feeling of nobody taking art seriously, a feeling of not being able to get my point across through galleries and museums. I don't really want to rebel against the rules of the art world. I rebel against the unjust things of the real world. The common people´s preconceptions of art are very neutralizing. If you listen to a dialog in a theater, the context and the knowledge of you knowing it´s art neutralizes a lot of things. But if you hear the same dialog in a city tram, you experience it in a very different way. It´s meaningful in a whole

"I think food companies are much more lethal than arms trade and drug industry."

other level, because it´s more real. I wanted to lose this alienating distance of art and make the educational experience stronger. This is why I wanted to hide the fact that it was an art project as long as possible, that´s why I invented the fictional terrorist group FLA.

Marx said politics is all about economics. Nowadays even people´s identities are about economics, about things they consume. We are living in consumerist times, people built their lives and identities around what they buy. Neoliberals buy their fancy brands, hippies buy their biodynamics, snowboarders buy their Oaklies and Red Bulls. We all have strong emotional relationships with brands, be it hate or love. And touching these products is sometimes like touching religious or national icons. It brings out the soft spots in our societies, in people. That´s why they are good tools to tell stories with.

The meaning people give to food is overwhelming. Food is in the core of religious ceremonies, national identities, everyday events, our health, politics and childhood memories. We cannot live without food, and still it´s so much more. And when all this is commercialized and branded, genetically manipulated and privatized, I see no way to avoid the topic of food. I think food companies are much more lethal than arms trade and drug industry. That´s the message FLA was trying to spread.

My favorite that you do is the Tony the Tiger campaign. It is fabulous. Could you tell me a bit about that and the response you received, both from individuals and the corporations that you screwed with?
What the *Tony Is Back!* films are trying to show is what happens when people obey blindly the dictates of their authorities. Our problem is that people are obedient all over the world in the face of poverty and starvation and stupidity, and war, and cruelty. Like Howard Zinn said, historically, the most terrible things—war, genocide, and slavery—have resulted not from disobedience, but from obedience. I think we are on the verge of something terrible, and if we don't say no now we might slide into it.

These films are ultimately supposed to be encouraging people and corporations to take responsibility of their actions and say no every time we see something unfair. The films are also the beginning of the story where after realizing he has done wrong, Tony the Tiger, the corporate cereal icon starts having doubts about his career and wants to do something more with his life than endorse sales.

The inspiration comes from way back. Twenty-five years ago, when I was twelve-years-old, Tony the Tiger was my superhero. Tony the Tiger helped me and other white middle-class kids all over the world to solve our every day problems in TV commercials. The Cold War had just ended and capitalism had suddenly won! Everyone was sure that a better world had arrived, there was going to be an eternal economical growth, and the billions we used on the arms race would balance our budgets, solve the problems of hunger, racism and inequality. The future seemed bright.

I was mesmerized by the way Tony tackled our problems with such power and confidence—that he claimed came from his vitamin packed Frosted Flakes cereal. He empowered us kids in situations where we doubted ourselves the most, in our middle-class hobbies like horseback riding, hockey or skiing down scary slopes, where bullies were always picking on our poor skills. Tony was our authority figure, our power animal that solved our problems with simple solutions. Once he was done we thought we will never need Tony again. We were going to be fine.

Oh boy, were we wrong. Now thirty years later not only we kids have grown up but also our problems have grown. On a global scale. To our great disappointment, this golden age of capitalism has been no less destructive. We are the first western generation in 100 years that is poorer and sicker than our parents. The end of Cold War didn't end repression, hunger, unemployment, racism, slavery or homelessness.

We need Tony now more than ever. We need Tony to feel powerful again. To know what to do when in doubt. Even though in the fourth film Tony is still confused about the scale and seriousness of our problems, he will in the end start teaching us proper ways to deal with them.

How long do you think it will be before our current system of capitalism collapses?
Something must happen soon, at least within my lifetime because if we continue doing nothing, the speed this system is emptying the environmental resources there will be nothing left change. I don't think even the capitalists want to become the rulers of cinder.

What are you up to next?
I am actually doing a longer film around the *Tony Is Back!* films, that tell a more elaborate story about the main characters in the films.

John Zerzan

JOHN ZERZAN is an influential author and lecturer on anarchism and primitivism. He finds most, if not all, systems that man has created to be inherently oppressive, and of course he is pretty much right about all that. His latest book is *Why Hope? The Stand Against Civilization*, which was published by Feral House.

You have been called an anarcho-primitivist, and an eco-anarchist. For the uninitiated, can you give us an idea of your worldview?

In sum, anarcho-primitivism is the conclusion that if the future isn't somehow primitive, there won't be a future. Every past civilization has failed and this one, the only one left, is rapidly on the road to self-destruction. The key force or ethos of civilization is domestication, starting with animals and plants and always going forward. It is control, ever deepening and extending, including nanotechnology and total surveillance. Free life disappears along with the health of the biosphere itself. This or that reform which does not tackle the nature of civilization, which is domestication, is superficial and futile.

In 1994 you wrote in your book *Future Primitive and Other Essays*, "Never before have people been so infantilized, made so dependent on the machine for everything; as the earth rapidly approaches its extinction due to technology, our souls are shrunk and flattened by its pervasive rule". How do you feel things have gone in the twenty years since then?

That quote is even more obviously valid now than it was in 1994. In fact the pace of the thing has increased. Extinction of species, empty lives, the whole pathological totality worsens. Now we have rampage shootings as an everyday phenomenon, rising chronic illnesses and suicide rates and a more and more poisoned physical environment, to mention just a bit of it. Hollow lives staring at screens, the sense of no future, the direction could not be more stark. Avoidance, denial are understandable given how bad it's getting but facing up to reality must happen.

"Our work
is not for
cynics or others
who prefer
surrender."

What do you consider the most positive aspects of a hunter-gatherer society as opposed to a modern one?
I think the main plus is that hunter-gatherer life was face-to-face. In band society people were accountable, had to take responsibility. Whereas in mass society we have the opposite. Today, because of, not despite technology, we are more and more isolated. Community, the fundamental aspect of non-domesticated and non-industrial life, is gone. Full stop. Hence the shootings, by unmoored individuals, belonging to nothing. Less work, too. Civilization means always more work, not to mention chronic war and the objectification of women.

I know you are probably a bit tired, or really tired, of talking about it, but can you touch on your relationship with Ted Kaczynski?
Kevin Tucker and I found Kaczynski making dishonest use of sources in his critique of anarcho-primitivism. That cannot be tolerated. One may think that anarcho-primitivism bases itself on faulty grounding but we try very hard to be scrupulous about the evidence, e.g. anthropological evidence. Bad faith blocks discourse about disagreements. Dialog is essential but some things prevent it.

You said in a recent interview your book, *Why Hope*, was addressing the "nihilism and retreat within the anarchist movement." Why should we care what happens to us, or the world at this point?
For those who don't care about themselves or the world, all ideas are irrelevant, eh? Our work is not for cynics or others who prefer surrender.

"I wanted to
get posts about weird
shit like communicating
with daemonic forms of
intelligence in people's
feeds right next to posts
about their friends' kids,
Buzzfeed quizzes,
and whatnot."

Thad McKraken

THAD McKRAKEN is a student of the occult who enjoys what he calls "ganjatating." He writes a lot, and well, for the website Disinfo.com. His latest book is *Transmissions From Outside of Time*. In it he writes of his ability to "contact extra-dimensional forms of intelligence by means of weed based sex magick."

You write that you were "summoned into the occult" can you tell me a little about that?

Yeah, it's a weird story. As a preface, I started playing around with Robert Monroe's techniques for astral projection when I was eighteen. Of course, I took an interest in all things high strangeness because for some reason or another I have an extremely strong reaction to drugs like psilocybin and LSD. What happens to me when I take those drugs is so unbelievably transcendent and indescribable it instantly piqued my interest in esoteric spirituality. After taking mushrooms for the first time I went from a dude with very little interest in spirituality to someone who obsessively read about things like shamanism, alien contact experiences, astral projection, and remote viewing, basically overnight.

So there was this point in my life ten years later, when I was twenty-eight, where I was self-destructing quite spectacularly. I was unemployed for a spell and because of that my drinking had gotten way out of control. I was also sleeping probably like twelve hours a day at least. So on one of these days while I was taking a midday pot nap when I probably should have been looking for work, a shrouded alien sorcerer dude showed up in my room and clapped his hands, much like how a hypnotist often awakens the people they've put in a trance: "clap clap." With that I bolted upright in my bed instantly and something deep within me had snapped. I suddenly realized that I'd been in complete denial about the supposed "reality" of the continual experiences I'd initiated by playing around with astral projection.

There was a war within me between the part of me that had been raised and educated in western materialist culture and the part of me that was communicating with the spirit world. I guess on a fundamental level I just couldn't accept this stuff because of my cultural conditioning and honestly wanted it to go away so I could be "normal." I mean, at that time I was even playing in a band with three other atheists, while simultaneously writing lyrics about advanced metaphysics and the spiritual ignorance of humanity. The guys in that band had absolutely no idea what I was even writing about. So once that entity clapped its hands I suddenly realized the problem. The war was over and the strangeness had won.

I immediately understood that I had psychic talents and that if I embraced them rather than continually questioning their "reality," they could be used to my advantage. And I had to start practicing magick. That was the other thing that was suddenly communicated to me quite clearly and I started casting sigils the next day. On an interesting note, from that day on my life turned around for the better fairly quickly. I transitioned to a more profitable and less demanding career and started dating the woman who'd become my future wife. All within a few months.

As I found out when I started writing about this stuff on the Internet, this makes me a bit unique among the magick crowd as I wasn't attracted to the dark spooky veneer that currently surrounds the occult in our culture, in fact, I sort of hate that stuff. I'd read about magick up to that point and it was the lameness of that façade that prevented me from pursuing it in the first place.

Organized religion has sort of ruined magick, and I honestly think if you go into this stuff with the attitude that you're summoning demons to be all Mr. Scary Monsters, it's just going to blow up in your face. I've now read countless stories online that confirm this. The reason has to do with the fact that focused intention works. If you intentionally try and summon negativity, it'll work and awful shit will happen. The real question is, why did you want to summon negativity into your life in the first place? You're trying to create your own reality with the power of your will and for some reason, you want your reality to be a horror movie? Why? Typically it's some deep-seated psychological problem.

Again, organized religion has turned this stuff into a complete joke, and if you read, say, Abramelin, he continually points out that he's doing the same sort of magick that Moses or Solomon was. So in the Bible, magickians are considered the heroes, but because of calculated religious propaganda, it's turned into "magickians are in the enemy." Aleister Crowley did not help this popular perception with his dumbass "I am the great beast 666" posturing... at all. In fact, the main reason we still talk about Crowley has to do with him being the one dude who was willing to play the role of the evil spooky villain Occultist that conservative Christianity wanted to sell. That's why he got so much press. If you read up on his life, the idea that he was some sort of master magickian is patently ridiculous, but hey, that's the power of modern myth making.

It seems that you use a lot of drugs. How do they help you open doors into the occult and your consciousness?

That's actually a bit of misnomer. I do smoke weed daily and I use psychedelics like psilocybin ritualistically maybe once a year at this point. Haven't done anything other than that in years. I don't even drink anymore because I literally can't. My body eventually became allergic to it and I get extremely hungover even after a drink or two. I am a vocal advocate of psychedelics though, because there's an enormous potentiality there for both communion with the divine and behavioral change. As mentioned, one psilocybin experience changed my behavior drastically as a teenager, not that I only did it once. The more you study psychology (which I do have a degree in), the more you realize that people build impenetrable ego-tunnels as they get older and it doesn't matter how many facts you present them with, there's no getting through to them. Psychedelics are maybe the best hope we have of breaking down those barriers and potentially facilitating behavioral change.

I talk about being an Occultist and into magick, but what I do has as much to do with shamanism as it does the occult. It largely involves tweaking the set and setting of the psychedelic experience to maximize potency. I started playing around with what I call auditory sorcery when I was nineteen or so as well. It's basically tweaking sound patterns in a calculated manner to summon the alien gods.

I'm also a huge advocate of what I call ganj-i-tation. I think weed can be used as a potent meditational aid, particularly when used in tandem with sex, and/or weird music. That's a concept that's been floating around in occult circles for centuries and tags back to the tantric practices of antiquity. What's mind blowing to me is that I seem to be the only one writing about this shit currently. I live in Seattle where marijuana is now legal, and I've literally not read a single other article about pot's potentiality as a spiritual tool written by anyone other than me. We've truly become that materialistic as a culture. We just look at it as "drugs fucking with your head" for purely recreational purposes these days. If you put a little effort into it, you can open up portals to other realms with that weed. Christ, that's where half our art comes from in the first place, we just don't conceptualize it that way.

You write a lot for disinfo.com, and it seems, people usually react in one of two ways: they think you are brilliant, or totally insane. How do you react to dealing with people who don't get what you do?

You forgot the third reaction, which is, you're going to hell because Jesus. I get that a lot. That's another thing that differentiates me from, say, most new age, psychedelic, or occult writers. I have that primal warrior DNA in me. I was sort of a pseudojock growing up and I've been lifting weights since I was fourteen. My grandpa was a judge and sort of a hardass and that sort of got passed down to me. I'm just one of those people that's not going to take other people's bullshit. What I love about weed in particular is that it really helps keep this part of me in check.

Fact is, people with alternative spiritual beliefs have been roughly the most discriminated against minority in history, and at some point we have to fight back if we want anything to change. I was arrested for possession of LSD when I was a college student and I still probably have a bit of a chip on my shoulder about that. I've done some very successful posts where I condescend to materialists in the exact same manner that I've been condescended to BY materialists for years. It's funny because I typically even point out that this is precisely what I'm doing right in these pieces. In general, people don't like being condescended to, and I find it hilarious that when I turn the tables it really pisses people off. That's precisely the point.

Fact is, materialism in general is going to end up on the wrong side of history. I write about all this weird shit like communicating with omni-dimensional forms of intelligence through sex magick, but truly, what I'm really saying is that none of this has been studied due to both religious and atheistic superstitions. It's literally been illegal to study psychedelic drugs for fifty years and we're slowly seeing some brave souls get that sort of research pushed through... finally. Reich's studies on orgone energy were literally made illegal as well. Imagine if it was illegal to study computers for fifty years. Modern psychiatry, outside of extreme cases, is essentially mind control at its very essence and largely junk science at best. Remote viewing has been demonstrated to work over and over again, yet we just pretend like it hasn't been. The implications of both of those fields of research are fairly paradigm-shattering and essentially point to the fact that all human consciousness is connected in ways we don't currently understand, because we've gone out of our way to NOT understand it. The entire rich history of human visionary experience has been edited out of all of our religious, academic, and media institutions for the most part. I'm just trying my best to edit it back in.

As for how I deal with the haters. Well, I mean, at times I was provoking them in the first place. The problem with getting engaged in these discussions is that it often backfires on you mentally by ruining your mood, so a lot of the time I avoid it. I also go in with the understanding that I literally don't have the ability to change these people's minds in most cases because that's not how human psychology works. They would have to have an experience that would lead them to change their minds. All I can do is point them in that direction. So I avoid confrontational comment section battles for the most part but chat with people who are more open to my ideas on my FB page constantly. I will say that this does depend on my mood. Sometimes I want to come after people. So be careful if you're posting negative comments on my shit, the possibility that I'm going to call you out is always there. To argue with me effectively you're going to have to somehow make the case that the best way to understand something like sex magick or astral projection is to know as little about it as possible because there's "nothing to know". It's not an easy argument to make. Good luck with that. Good luck out-writing me, too.

Tell me a little bit about your new book.
It's called *Transmissions From Outside of Time* and it's about the process of knowledge and conversation that I initiated with what classic occultists would refer to as my Holy Guardian Angel. It's sort of a year in the psychic life thing. When my writing first got picked up by Disinfo.com (which was a week after December 21, 2012, I might point out). I started not only documenting these transmissions, but posting them publicly on Facebook. I was doing this to fuck with Facebook primarily as it had turned into a bastion of bland safe for work discourse. I wanted to get posts about weird shit like communicating with daemonic forms of intelligence in people's feeds right next to posts about their friends' kids, Buzzfeed quizzes, and whatnot.

It was also an opportunity to finally keep a dream journal, which is something I'd always wanted to do but had never gotten around to. So I started doing it publicly. I might be the first person in history to do this I might point out. I had zero plans of turning this stuff into a book, but it got so fucking strange the notion eventually occurred to me. The strangest part is that whatever I was communicating with ended up predicting the future in quite "impossible" ways on multiple occasions. Since these things were all posted publicly before they happened, it's sort of hard to argue with. So the book is detailing that as I didn't even know it was happening at the time.

In general I was always amused with the classic hippy idea of turning oneself into living art, as laid out in say the book *The Electric Kool Aid Acid Test*. I pretty effectively did that as it's an amusing book that reads like surrealist fiction even though it's entirely autobiographical. It's also a direct assault on the materialistic interpretation of dreams in general. It's difficult to read and come away thinking "dreams are just random recounting of daily events", which was the dominant theory in regards to dreams I was taught as a psychology student. At some point we're going to have to recognize that dreams are direct communication with the spirit world, but we have a hard time understanding them because they're communicating in a subjective and metaphorical language we're sort of culturally programmed to not understand.

What is life like for you when you aren't doing your thing with writing, the occult or tripping people out?

That's sort of the funny thing. If I didn't write about the crazy shit that's going on in my psychic life, you'd never know any of it was happening. It's all occluded. On the surface I'm just a normal married dude working a soul draining corporate job he hates. I do make weird music and art, but in general, if you were to look at my life without seeing the occluded inner shit, most of it would be mind-numbingly boring. I'm a huge sports fan. No really, I'm completely obsessed with the NBA and I think I've watched every Seahawks game over the last four years except maybe two. As mentioned, I don't even drink anymore. Haven't stayed out all night snorting blow or blissing out on Ecstasy in nearly a decade. Haven't cheated on my wife once. I work out obsessively. I have a pug and like to take long walks with him on the beach. It's total dullsville.

Dennis Dechaine

DENNIS DECHAINE was incarcerated for the murder of Sarah Cherry, a twelve-year-old girl from Bowdoinham, Maine. Her body was found two days after she disappeared from her home while baby-sitting. He was convicted in 1989. He maintains his innocence. In the case of Dechaine there are a lot of people who believe him, including the Innocence Project, which has helped secure many new trials and exonerations for wrongfully convicted prisoners.

It's been a while since I have read anything about you. What is going on with you now?
I am currently preparing to file a writ of habeas corpus. I am trying to prove that crime scene DNA excludes me as Sarah Cherry's killer, that time of death also excludes me, and that the state's wanton incineration of crime scene evidence had left me at a disadvantage, legally speaking.

How is life in prison at this point?
I live in a prison where acts of violence per annum easily exceed the prison population. Not once in twenty-eight years of incarceration have I deigned to engage in such nonsense. For that matter I can make the same claim for the prior thirty years of my existence, a tragic irony when you consider I'm incarcerated for life for the brutal murder of a child.

I know this question might be a little trite, but what is it like for you being imprisoned for a crime that you say you did not commit?
Thinking about it can drive me to despair, as it should you. The tragedy of a perfectly nonviolent man languished in prison for a crime he didn't commit is dwarfed by the horrifying reality that the perpetrator is still living among you. Rest assured that I will never stop trying to correct the state's blunder.

Do you get treated differently in there as someone who many consider innocent?

"...the state's wanton incineration of crime scene evidence had left me at a disadvantage, legally speaking."

I assume that supporters and detractors are divided the same way as in the free world. How a person is treated in here is more a function of how he treats others and how he carries himself. I am not different than any other man. I try to make the world a better place through my actions, helping others when I can. I maintain friendships through phone calls, letters and visits and participate daily in family dynamics. I get up every morning go to work and do the best job I can, taking pride in what I produce in our industries program. I learn something new every day, either from my work or reading. I try hard to keep what is between my ears as healthy and fruitful as possible.

What were you doing before all this happened? Do you remember that day?

As for what I was doing before my arrest I had just come home to my Bowdoinham home after having enjoyed a family reunion. On the farm I was in the process of laying a foundation for a new greenhouse, and was excited about expanding the farm. Other than my unwarranted lack of freedom, perhaps my greatest sadness stems from the loss of potential imposed by fences and razor wire. That loss, Brian, is as much yours as it is mine.

"When you
begin to lift
off the ground
there is the sensation
of your skin separating
from your muscle,
sometimes there is a
burning sensation as you
settle into the hooks..."

Belle Vendetta

BELLE VENDETTA is a professional dominatrix, a sex educator,
a writer, a chef, a pole dancer, an activist and a fashion designer.
She also hangs her body from hook pierced through her flesh
as a member of the International Suspension Alliance.

I **first heard of suspension through RE/Search's *Modern Primitives* book, and Fakir Musafar. How did you first become involved in suspension?**

I first saw suspension in the film *A Man Called Horse*, but never imagined it would really be anything I would do or include in my life. I later got more comfortable around the idea from being involved in bmezine.com and IAMbmezine (a now mostly defunct social networking site for folks involved in body modification). At the time I was friends with a very teenaged Emrys Yetz, who is the founding member of Rites of Passage Suspension Group. He was planning a small event suspending a few people in his backyard and wondered if I was interested in coming to film it, which of course I said yes to. So that was the first time I ever saw it in person; it was very different from what I had imagined. Everyone was calm, there was tons of love and trust in the air, tears and hugs. I thought it was beautiful, but never thought of it as something I would personally do. It became something I thought about more and more and within a few months I was planning my first suspension with a few close friends. It only took that one time to really change my life and suspension became something really important to me. Before too long I was being trained to pierce and rig and began helping to plan even bigger events and became a member of Rites of Passage.

What is the International Suspension Alliance all about?

Suspension is something that crosses many borders. There are organized teams and events worldwide, with some big events each year that teams save up to travel to. Mainly Dallas Suscon in TX and the Oslo Suscon in Norway. For over a decade there's been talk about some sort of umbrella organization. A way to connect, share knowledge and network to be able to grow the suspension community in a safe and organized way. It's been a slow process and is still very much in the works. But I think it's a really positive thing to get the best team leaders and practitioners in our community together.

I know it may be hard to describe, but what does it feel like to be hanging from hooks?

It's really sort of impossible to describe and has so many variables, it wouldn't do it justice to try and give a generalized description of the feeling. It depends on what type of suspension you are doing, from what part of your body, your purposes for doing it. A chest suspension feels a lot different than a suicide suspension (from the back). It also depends on placement of hooks, number of hooks, gauge of hooks. Getting pierced well, feels like getting pierced. It hurts. I'm sure some folks would agree and find it enjoyable. When you begin to lift off the ground there is the sensation of your skin separating from your muscle, sometimes there is a burning sensation as you settle into the hooks and become comfortable. After the burning subsides and your endorphins have kicked in… free is the only word to describe it.

What kind of range of responses have you had from people that have tried this?

Every person has a different reaction. Everyone has a different reason for wanting to suspend. For some it's for spiritual and religious reasons, as a ritual, some for an art project, some for the endorphin release, and just about every reason in between, Some folks don't even get off the ground. They find the pain too intense to be able to let go. Some people get off the ground and immediately begin smiling and laughing, some people cry uncontrollably. In my decade-plus of helping people fly however, I have NEVER heard anyone say they regretted the experience.

What else do you do in life other than suspension work?

I write! I get to do metal and rock interviews and reviews, write about feminism, sex work and even about body modification and suspension. I am a professional Dominatrix, and award winning adult star, a social justice warrior and a dancer. I dance burlesque and pole dance and feature at gentlemen's clubs. I also have a past life as a chef and sometimes still dabble with catering and creating fine dishes. I have a pretty varied life, it's never boring that's for sure.

Kristian Williams

KRISTIAN WILLIAMS is an anarchist and an author. He is not a big fan of cops. His book, *Our Enemies in Blue: Police and Power in America*, was published by Soft Skull Press and is available in over 500 libraries.

Your book is extremely critical of the police. What does the police department of the United States represent to you?

The police are specialists in coercive force. Their distinguishing characteristic is the combination of surveillance and violence to make people do what people with power want them to do. That usually gets described in terms of enforcing the law, but what I found in my research is that the real distribution of power is a much better indicator of how the police will act in any given situation. On the whole, they behave in ways that serve the interests of the powerful at the expense of the rest of us.

To me, a police officer's main job is to keep things the way they are "supposed to be." In your opinion, is the job of the police force to stop crime, or to control the working class?

Well, both, but the latter is more important. In fact, what gets counted as "crime" is generally class-coded. The disorderly behaviors of poor people get criminalized, while wealthy people see their misdeeds sanctified by the law, or handled as administrative matters, or—when they are considered criminal—met with loose enforcement and light penalties. So, sleeping under a bridge is a crime, but evicting poor people from their housing is just good business.

Of course it's not just class. The police also work hard to maintain our society's racial hierarchy. Racial profiling affects people of color of all classes, limits their geographic (and therefore social) mobility, and so serves to marginalize them. And, interestingly, every reputable study has shown that it has no use in terms of fighting crime. It is purely a matter of preserving white supremacy.

"...violence is inherent to policing. They're trained for it, armed for it, authorized to use it."

You argue that acts of police brutality and violence are not aberrations, but are in fact the norm. Can you expand on this at all?

I devote an entire chapter to this question in the book, but the short version is that violence is inherent to policing. They're trained for it, armed for it, authorized to use it. Their institutional culture supports it and to some degree their collective self-perception is centered on it. Viewed at the level of the institution, it is a routine aspect of police work, even if the average officer uses violence rather rarely. The question of how much of that violence is legitimate and how much is abusive is a normative one; it depends on questions of law, policy, ethics, and social expectation. But the point is, if you institutionalize violence in this way, it is fairly certain that the members of the institution will sometimes exceed the purported limits. Looked at that way, even the excesses are part of the normal functioning of the institution.

Are there any solutions to this issue? Where do you see things going if this doesn't change?

In the short term, I think it is worth pursuing reforms that make the police more accountable and that limit their access to violence. In the long term, I think we need to abolish this institution and find some better means of ensuring public safety. Since the police are both a product and a protector of social inequality, the abolitionist project requires an entirely different kind of society, one characterized by a radical egalitarianism. Of course it is impossible at this stage to know exactly what that will look like, and it's hard to see how we could get there from where we are at present. That doesn't make it any less pressing, however. The only real check on power is popular resistance. Without it, things inevitably get worse.

"I used to get several hundred pounds of weed at a time and like 100 sheets of LSD. I used to visit the different colleges my friends attended. It was like have drugs will travel."

Seth Ferranti

SETH FERRANTI is an author, the creator of a true crime comic
book, and a former LSD kingpin who started writing while
in prison. He was once among the top fifteen most wanted
fugitives on the U.S Marshalls most wanted list, and has spent
twenty-one years in prison. He writes regularly for Vice.com.

Can you tell me a little bit about what you were doing that got you
sent to prison in the first place?

I was selling LSD and marijuana at fifteen colleges in five states on
the East Coast from 87–91. I wasn't a big drug dealer but for a kid I was doing
good. I used to get several hundred pounds of weed at a time and like 100
sheets of LSD. I used to visit the different colleges my friends attended. It was
like have drugs will travel.

**Three-hundred-and-four months is a mind blowing sentence for a twenty-
two-year-old dealing some acid and some weed, I know there is no way to
really fully describe this, but where were you at emotionally and mentally
when you were sent to prison?**

I was fucked up for real. I was self-medicating though. Smoking marijuana every
day. Even in prison. So I was numbing myself. But I was angry, I was frustrated.
I was almost like how can my country do this to me? But you get over it, you
adapt, you survive. I channeled all my negative energy into sports and working
out and getting college degrees and writing. That was how I found my peace.

**How were you able to start writing and get your work out there in public
while in prison?**

It was a long and involved process. I used to find editors' names on the
mastheads of magazines I liked along with their addresses. I would write them
and pitch them my ideas and my story. I would even write articles and make
100 photocopies and send that same article out to 100 different publications. I
did this for years and bombarded all these magazines' mailrooms with letters.

Dudes in the joint used to see me and couldn't fathom why I was sending out so much mail. Sometimes like 500 letters a month. I was promoting myself and my work. I got some people interested and that led to the next thing and the next thing and so on.

Can you tell me a little about the community in prison, and what that little society was like, as opposed to what people think it was like?
Prison is this little pseudoworld where you get big respect for being violent or for having a lot of time in prison. There is a twisted sense of honor or convict mentality that everyone adheres to. It's really boring and to be honest sucks but you have to deal with it and play the game. I became an expert at doing time and being a convict but when I came home I adjusted my mentality because although that mentality helped me to thrive in there I knew I had to lose it to survive in the real world.

You're out... what is life about for you now?
Life is about living each day to its fullest and getting my projects off. I have lots of ideas and my art is my life. I just keep plugging a long and executing. I got my comic line coming out this year, working on some documentaries and film stuff and I got a lot of other stuff in the works. Trying to make up for lost time and become a player doing what I love to do—playing make believe.

Nick Devin

Nothing—and I mean *nothing*—pisses off people more than a pedophile. Even one that has never done anything wrong. So it is no wonder that NICK DEVIN is a pseudonym. He is one of the men behind virtuouspedophiles.com

Can you tell me a little bit about what Virtual Pedophiles is all about?

We really have two goals: (1) to reduce child sexual abuse, and (2) to help non-offending pedophiles lead productive, happy lives. These goals really work hand in hand as research shows that pedophiles are most likely to molest children when they are depressed, alone and isolated from their communities.

There are a number of things that we do to try to accomplish these goals. We run a support group where we provide advice to one another on various topics. Older members who have lived with pedophilia for a long time can advise younger members on how to remain offense free. Some of our members suffer from self-hate and depression as a result of their pedophilia. This can be quite debilitating. We try to tell them that having pedophilic feelings is not a moral condition; it is an unfortunate result of biology and possibly early childhood experiences. No one is sexually attracted to children because they choose to be sexually attracted to children. Who would choose such a thing? And people who are sexually attracted to children can't stop being sexually attracted to children. But people who are unfortunate enough to be sexually attracted to children can choose not to interact sexually with a child. We believe pedophiles that successfully resist their attractions should take pride in that, as opposed to feeling shame for having feelings that they didn't choose to have.

We also interact a fair amount with the general public to educate them about the existence of non-offending pedophiles. The stigma attached to pedophilia is counter-productive; it causes pedophiles to remain hidden as opposed to coming forward to obtain therapeutic treatment that might be needed to help a pedophile lead a happy, productive, law-abiding life. We find that when people are able to

"...we didn't choose to be sexually attracted to children and can't stop being sexually attracted to children, but that many of us successfully resist our sexual feelings..."

understand the distinction between pedophilia (sexual feelings for children) and child sexual abuse (interacting sexually with a child), and they understand that many pedophiles successfully resist their sexual feelings, the hatred goes away.

Finally, we interact a fair amount with leading professional groups such as the Association for Treatment of Sexual Abusers, in an effort to make therapists more accepting of non-offending pedophiles. Many therapists have a visceral "yuck" reaction when seeing a pedophile, which makes treatment impossible. We have access to the ATSA list of professionals, and we are often able to refer pedophiles to sympathetic therapists near where they live.

How many people do you guys hear from on a monthly basis, and are most of the people folks that have not acted out yet?
We have had slightly more than 1,500 people sign up for our support group. Some get what they need and leave, some don't like us and leave, some stay a very long time. Typically about 200–250 people will post in our support group in a given month. We have a few members who admit to having offended in the past, and are committed to not doing so again. I don't know the actual number, but I would guess it to be fewer than five.

I know this question might seem obvious, but what is it like to be judged for what you are thinking as opposed to what you actually do?
I think most people who judge us harshly do so because they simply are not aware of the existence of non-offending pedophiles. Telling them the truth—that we didn't choose to be sexually attracted to children and can't stop being sexually attracted to children, but that many of us successfully resist our sexual feelings, causes many people to view us less harshly.

Of course some will still hate—either because they think we'll eventually molest a kid or because they think they should hate anyone who has sexual feelings towards children, whether they act on those sexual feelings or not. With respect to those who think we'll eventually molest a kid, there's really no way to prove we won't, just like they can't ever prove that they won't rape an adult sometime in the future. All we can say is we haven't done it yet, and we won't, which is all they could say if asked to prove they won't rape another adult. As for those who want to hate us just because we have the attraction, all we can say is what I said above. We didn't choose to be sexually attracted to children and can't stop being sexually attracted to children, but we can and have successfully resisted our sexual feelings. If they think that makes us worthy of hate, so be it.

I once wrote an article suggesting that if pedophiles felt less shame they might be able to get help before they offend—and a lot of people got extremely angry. Why do you think just the very thought of helping

someone that is a pedophile angers some people so much?

One of the things that has surprised me since forming Virtuous Pedophiles is how rare it is that we get hate mail. I'll bet we haven't had more than ten hateful emails over the three or four years that we've been doing this. By contrast, we've received many times that number of supportive emails from non-pedophiles, including from former victims of childhood sexual abuse. Many have commented that they'd wished that we were around when they were kids, so that maybe their abusers would have received support that might have prevented their abuse. So I would hope that you would have received some supporting emails in addition to the angry ones.

As for the angry ones, one criticism that we have received is that we are trying to "normalize" pedophilia, to make it ok for pedophiles to have sex with children. Of course we say precisely the opposite, that pedophiles should not have sex with children. We do try to humanize pedophiles, to make people see us as human beings with a difficult problem that we have to deal with. Maybe the angry comments that you received results from the same confusion—that people see your article as trying to normalize pedophilia, as opposed to trying to humanize it.

When you don't act on things does it get easier with time, or is it something that never really goes away?

The sexual attraction to children does not go away, though sex drive tends to go down as you get older. Self-control increases, so it gets easier to avoid sexual interaction with children.

Matt Campbell

MATT CAMPBELL thinks men get a raw deal and does his best to shine a light on all of the injustices that men face. He is the editor of the Men's Activists News Network (MANN). Whose purpose is to "To provide pro-male activists with news and information that will aid them in working toward establishing equal rights for men and the improvement of men's lives."

Tell me a little bit about what Mensactivism.org does.
MANN is a men's rights news and interests dissemination website. It runs relevant and of-interest stories from the news, reports, press releases from MR organizations and others, as well as announces and publicizes opportunities for MR collaboration and activism. MANN maintains editorial independence by not accepting donations nor running any kinds of advertisements.

What do you think the biggest issues are that men are dealing with today?
Probably the single biggest problem men face is misandry itself, because it is misandry entrenched in today's western social culture that fuels and permits many forms of anti-male legislation, double standards, and hostile and prejudicial attitudes. From these arise the many specific problems men face in different contexts, including anti-male bigotry on college campuses, in government policy, in courts of law, and even in business policies. These are heads of the Hydra, by analogy. The Hydra itself is misandry (paired with nymph tropism) which gives rise to the specific problems that men face.

If I were to pick the top three heads of the Hydra in terms of priority of concern, they would be anti-father child custody dispute bias, de facto presumed guilt in courts of law and the court of public opinion due to male gender, and anti-male discrimination in schools of higher learning in the form of the misuse and misapplication of Title IX (here in the U.S.). (But there are plenty of other heads on the Hydra, too, and others may have different ideas around which are most important.) These are just three big ones.

"Men are seen by both sexes as "appropriate" targets of violence when the assailant is moved to anger or if they have a "good enough" reason."

I saw on your website you wrote a bit about how it was a myth that men were more violent than women. Can you expand on that?

To be careful about words, "violence" has in some circles come to be defined quite expansively to include even such things as disagreeing with another person. I think this is ludicrous, so to be clear, I use "violence" in the more common sense, meaning to use physical force, with or without an instrument or weapon, with intent to hurt/injure/kill against another person.

Numerous studies have shown that women are as likely (or more likely) to initiate DV [domestic violence] as much as men. They are also more likely to use a weapon or instrument when assaulting their partners, be those partners male or female. The MANN site has references to just some of these studies. As to other violence, most recorded acts of non-DV violence are indeed done by men, but largely against other men. Men are seen by both sexes as "appropriate" targets of violence when the assailant is moved to anger or if they have a "good enough" reason. In contrast, both sexes are admonished that at no time should a female be the target of violence. No such messages about men along these lines get taught; in fact, just the opposite. Instead, children and adults alike should be getting admonished against using violence against another person, period, no matter the supposed justification offered for it.

Do you have anything in place to help men falsely accused of domestic violence or rape? How often do you think this type of thing occurs?

It's hard to state how frequent false DV/rape accusations occur because they exist whether or not the falsehood of the accusation is revealed. While some people come up with statistics about rape victims, for example, based on extrapolations or just plain guesses, that isn't a valid approach to formulating statistics, especially when they are promulgated as facts, more so when by our government officials.

What is known is that contrary to some people's assertions, false accusations of DV/rape are not nearly as rare or exceptional as claimed. One thing that is obvious is that there are rewards for leveling false DV (or rape) claims, especially in child custody dispute cases. This isn't to say any given accusation in a custody case is false. It simply acknowledges that it is usable as a means to try to get an upper hand in the case or to serve as a distraction from other matters. False accusations can be motivated by other things: revenge after a break-up, a power play within a relationship, a desire for attention, etc. However even when an accusation is shown to be false, the typical case sees no punishment against the false accuser. This is an example of nymph tropism at work in the legal system. Unless and until the law punishes false accusers, false accusations will continue to be a problem for men in legal and other contexts.

As for resources for men falsely accused, a small number of attorneys specialize in taking on false accusations. However to the best of my knowledge, there are no organizations that offer free or discount legal services to help men combat false accusations specifically. There may be discount legal service firms or agencies (e.g.: The Legal Aid Society) that might help a man (or woman) dispute a false accusation, but such groups don't specialize in them nor are they likely to prioritize such cases. They have more of other kinds to pursue that won't require as many resources, such as divorces and landlord-tenant disputes.

Obviously you know that a lot of women out there think that websites like yours are ridiculous, and even hurtful. How would you respond to that?
The best thing to say to women (and men) who dismiss the MRM or MANN in particular is to go to the site (and other MRM sites) and start reading. If after doing some investigating, a person doesn't believe MRAs have a point, then they are entitled to their opinions. However if anyone thinks merely because they disagree with or don't like the MRM cause that it won't grow or that MRAs will stop being MRAs to suit their opinions, they are wrong. Just as feminists are unlikely to stop being feminists merely because MRAs disagree with the more unsavory tenets of their ideology (which include the killing off/engineering the die-off of most human males—no joke), neither feminists nor non-feminists should expect MRAs to drop the cause simply because one or more others find it disagreeable.

There is a lot of misandry in today's culture and it pops up in overt and covert ways on TV, radio, in politics, in legal decisions, and in ordinary conversations. These actions not only reinforce misandry and promulgate its effects, but also help bring more and more MRAs into existence. In my case, one day after hearing someone for the thousandth time say something misandrist, I had had it. I started Googling "men's rights" and went from there. So for anyone who likes to indulge in sexist and/or racist anti-male bigotry, I say, keep it up. You are only creating more converts to the MRM cause. We're here until the hatred, bigotry, and injustices end.

Seth Leaf Pruzansky

SETH LEAF PRUZANSKY is an author and an entrepreneur. He was
sentenced to prison for nearly five years for running a large-scale
marijuana business. Now he owns the bottled water company
Tourmaline Sping. He says his water "is so naturally pure it exceeds
every Federal and State guideline for drinking water straight from
the ground." His memoir is currently being shopped to publishers.

**I know that you also were involved pretty heavily with heroin for a
while. What should the government do with people who are arrested
for drug offenses, or should there even be drug offenses?**
As an enterprising entrepreneur I had always been looking to engage in
profitable ventures. Having been raised in a "pot culture," and living in a state
(Maine) with a very liberal attitude towards marijuana, it was often times too
easy for me to sell it. And usually I didn't sell just a little bit, I sold a lot of it.

In my younger years I really believed in the social and political liberation of
marijuana legalization. But as I grew older I stopped caring about it for many
different reasons. Most of them were based on my own opinions and personal
observations of how marijuana was abused. I didn't want to contribute to that.

Even though my heart wasn't really in it, I continued to sell it because it was
so easy. I believe this is in good part what led me to getting arrested.

**How did you feel then, and how do you feel now, about being sent to
prison for such a long time for selling marijuana?**
Getting arrested, indicted, waiting on pretrial for a year and then getting a five-
year sentence for selling marijuana was certainly one of the biggest nightmares
of my life at the time. When it happened you couldn't have found a bigger baby
or victim on the planet. I was also really physically ill and so I subscribed to the
belief that my life had been ruined.

While doing time in federal prison I suffered tremendously for the first half
of the sentence. But as I sat and faced my demons hour after hour, day after
day, night after night, week after week, month after month and year after year, I

"I literally transitioned from being the biggest victim on the planet to becoming empowered in a way that I had only dreamed about."

began to find a clarity of perceptive observation that I hadn't known since I was a child. I was able to see beyond the scope of how my life experience appeared to me at that time and truly come to embrace a deeper meaning inherent within the prison experience itself.

I literally transitioned from being the biggest victim on the planet to becoming empowered in a way that I had only dreamed about. I was then able to observe reality from a universal observation point that provided great inner peace.

You are shopping a book now about your experiences, how did the prison experience change you?

The prison experience in itself didn't necessarily change me but it absolutely provided the framework for me to begin taking action steps towards changing myself. And that is exactly what I did. As brutal as my environment was at that time I fully realized that in my life outside of prison I would not have as much time to focus on my own inner self-development. I treated my time there as a monastic and extended meditation retreat. I literally spent hours meditating every day. It was certainly some of the most difficult but most rewarding work I had ever done. A year and a half went by of me doing this every day and I saw no results. But then, almost like magic everything shifted. Suddenly even though I was physically incarcerated, spiritually I was free.

It became ironic but completely understandable how having my body and mind physically incarcerated would allow me the opportunity to practice setting my spirit free. It was the perfect recipe for success in that regard.

The book I wrote was part of this process. I initially wrote it as a way to look for limiting patterns in my own life. I started from birth and went to the moments of my incarceration. I became literarily aware of patterns that were holding me back—limiting stories I incessantly told myself. This awareness provided the fuel for me to step outside of these patterns and not allow them to rule me anymore.

Can you tell me a little bit about what you were doing that led you to be sent to prison?

In my late teens I was offered heroin and incredibly my body rejected it to the degree that I thought I'd never try it again, but somehow I did. Before I knew it I was trapped in a full-fledged addiction where my every waking moment was consumed by either doing the drug or figuring out how to get more of it.

It took a number of overdoses before I realized that if I continued to do it, it would kill me. My will to live was so much stronger than my will to not live, so I made a choice and a commitment to that choice, to kick for good. The excruciating mental, emotional, physical and spiritual pain that followed immediately after I kicked was absolutely harder than the entire prison experience. But I had no one to blame for that other than myself, so I took full responsibility for cleaning up. That was twenty years ago.

The issue of what the government or society should do about drug addiction is very complicated because all the treatment or all the punishment in the world won't make a difference to the addicted individual who doesn't want to change. Almost everyone I knew who was addicted to heroin either died, went to prison for a long time, is still doing some form of opiate or if they managed to get clean they are seriously addicted to something else with severe mental/emotional issues to boot.

I have seen so many full-blown addicts go through deeply traumatic rock bottom experiences and still not want to change. The very few who have are the ones who underwent heavy duty hallucinogenic experiences (usually in Ayahuasca or Peyote ceremonies) or those who had some sort of "spiritual awakening" where they realized that the essence of what they are is way more than just the human personality who they think they are.

If we as a culture can get addicts to a deeper place of self-realization, to see beyond the bounds of the way things appear to be with our "normal" senses and to see into the heart of the great mystery that life truly is—than those individuals will usually begin taking steps to clean themselves up. Because at that point they then know how precious life really is and that it's really not theirs to waste.

What is life like for you now?
My personal life is incredible now. But I have had to earn it. I take all that I know and am using it to spiritually effectuate the world to a critical mass of great awaking. I do this because I know both the value of what's at stake and the potential beauty that is possible. Deep in my heart or soul I believe that we will awaken to the truth of life as a species—even if it doesn't look that way right now!

John Marmyz

JOHN MARMYZ is an author and a professor of philosophy
at the university at Marin. He is also a practicing nihilist. He
is the author of numerous books about nihilism, his latest
is a novel, which is appropriately titled *The Nihilist*.

I have to say, it was hard for me to find a nihilist to interview for this book. Can you tell me a bit about how you got involved in this philosophy?

It doesn't surprise me that you've had difficulty finding a self-proclaimed nihilist to interview. The term "nihilism," which literally means "a doctrine of nothingness," traditionally has been used as a term of criticism or even derision. It's usually intended as an insult rather than as a badge of pride. This unfavorable usage originated with attacks against Kantian philosophy in the eighteenth century. Because Kant denied the possibility of anything but subjective knowledge of reality, his critics complained that he had reduced the objective world to nothing. Thus, he was a nihilist; and that was not supposed to be a good thing! The negative connotations of the term were only amplified when Russian revolutionaries in the nineteenth century adopted it as a name for their own movement, which actively pursued political violence through bombings, assassinations, and general mayhem. Today, the term is probably most often associated with Friedrich Nietzsche, a philosopher who also is viewed in a negative light by many folks because of his unwitting influence on the Nazis.

I have to admit that all of this negative press is partially responsible for my interest in nihilism. It was when I was a teenager that I first heard the word, and the very sound of it resonated with a kind of mysterious danger that I found alluring. Couple this with the fact that the music I listened to and the books and movies I consumed were often condemned by mainstream media critics for peddling "nihilistic" messages and it was perhaps inevitable that I was drawn to explore this dark area of philosophy. I guess my thinking was that if the art I like truly is nihilistic (as the critics claimed), then there must be something nihilistic about me.

"...if our life on this planet is all that there is, then there is no heavenly reward, nor is there any hellish punishment, when you die. And we all die. So what is the point of it all?"

In high school, I read Stanley Rosen's *Nihilism: A Philosophical Essay* and understood almost none of it! However, one thing that the book did teach me is that nihilism is a much more complicated issue than most critics make it out to be. It is a worldview that cannot easily be dismissed with an arrogant and condescending wave of the hand. As I explored the philosophy further, I progressively became more and more clear about how correctly it describes my own experiences in the world.

Through my late teens and twenties, I continued to develop my understanding of nihilism while singing in a punk rock band, participating in underground publishing, serving in the Army, and studying philosophy. Eventually, I earned my Ph.D. and wrote a dissertation on the topic that was published as *Laughing at Nothing: Humor as a Response to Nihilism*. In a sense I guess you could say that my entire life so far has been an attempt to articulate what nihilism is and why I am proud to call myself a nihilist.

It seems to me rather obvious that our lives have no real meaning or value. We all die and what we do here on Earth means nothing. Why do you think it bugs people out so much to admit that?
I think you've put your finger on one of the central issues of concern to nihilists: human finitude. If, as Nietzsche proclaimed, "God is dead," then our life on this planet is all that there is. And if our life on this planet is all that there is, then there is no heavenly reward, nor is there any hellish punishment, when you die. And we all die. So what is the point of it all?

If you think of meaning or value as something that exists objectively, "out there" in the world independent of human thought, the nihilist claims that you are out of luck. Objective truth, meaning and value are illusions; mental projections that we reify and then imagine to be separate and independent of us. Thus, according to the nihilist, values, meaning, morality, and truth itself are all tied to the human perspective; and if they are tied to the human perspective, then like humans they are impermanent and fleeting. When we die, they die with us.

However, for most people, "real" things can't be fleeting, impermanent or transitory. They have to be stable, permanent, and unchanging. Think about how people talk about "true" love, for instance. A "true" love is one that doesn't change from day to day. It is one that lasts forever. So when nihilists reject the objective existence of absolutes, they are undermining the very ground upon which many people base their lives, loves, and hopes about the world. To claim that values and meaning are human created projections endangers confidence in the highest, most holy ideals and, so the critics claim, puts us on a dangerous road to relativism, which in turn can lead to atrocity, immorality, and emptiness. This, I think, is what really bugs people out. They worry, as Dostoevsky suggests, that if God is dead, then anything is permitted.

Most people think that nihilists are out to destroy, and don't care about life, that to be a nihilist means that one is angry in a certain sense. Personally the fact that I believe in nothing makes me feel at peace with things and makes me calm. Can you shed some light on that thought process?

In my view, it is the people who believe in objective absolutes that have done the most damage to the world. They are the ones who have the arrogance to believe that the imperfect nature of our world can somehow be repaired, and that they are wise enough to know exactly how to do so. Historically, they are the ones who have been the most willing to kill, maim and torture in the name of ideals that they think are universal and absolute.

While there is nothing in nihilism that prevents apathy or destruction or anger, neither is there anything in it that necessitates these things. Nietzsche makes a distinction between active and passive forms of nihilism. The active nihilist is one who strikes out at the void, rebelling against the meaningless of the universe. This can sometimes culminate in angry violence and destruction. The passive nihilist, on the other hand, withdraws from the world, seeing action as pointless, useless. This can sometimes culminate in apathy or despair. However, active nihilism can also result in bursts of artistic creativity, acts of charity, or pure adventure. If one feels released from the bonds of absolutes—if anything is permitted—liberation and a sense of freedom might be the result. Indeed, even passive nihilism may have a positive side, as it can result in the promotion of modesty and the dismantling of human arrogance. By highlighting our finitude, it can remind us that in the grand scheme of things we are not that important, thus encouraging us not to overestimate our place in the universe.

I agree with the philosopher Martin Heidegger who stated that in its essence, there is nothing negative about nihilism. It is a perspective that can potentially lead to all sorts of consequences—both positive and negative—just like any other philosophy.

This might be a tad simplistic, but why do you think people care about things that mean absolutely nothing? Why do you think people allow gods, jobs, leaders and politicians to have so much power?

I think that traditional values, religion and the conventions of society comprise a kind of herd ideology that is very attractive for those who have no desire or inclination to get drawn into the endlessly deep pit of individual philosophical thought. Most people are probably more concerned with being happy than they are with confronting difficult truths, and so in order to reduce the amount of friction in their lives they buy into the ready-made systems that are a part of mainstream culture. By worshiping the right god, working hard at the right job, supporting the right politicians, wearing the right clothes, driving the right kind of car and watching the right kinds of TV shows, people come to feel that they have a role to play in the system and that the world has a purpose. Everything makes sense. Everything is in its place. It is clear what is right and what is wrong. And this makes people comfortable and happy.

But ready-made herd ideologies don't come from nowhere. They have to be developed and built up over time by concrete human beings who, bit by bit, collect together and consolidate their beliefs into systems of values, norms and expectations. These systems eventually become solidified into the sorts of cultural and societal "truths" that are taught in schools, preached in the pulpit, and voted into law. People eventually forget that none of these "truths" are actually inscribed in nature, and so when someone like a pesky nihilist comes along and questions the value of the "system," or starts to demand some sort of justification for religious belief, or starts to propose alternative views on reality, people feel threatened, and in consequence the herd they are a part of becomes defensive.

The defensiveness of the herd often results in the persecution—and sometimes in the execution—of freethinking, individual philosophers. It's been going on for thousands of years, from Socrates to Snowden. Most people, no matter what the time period, prefer comfortable illusions to difficult realities since such illusions offer a stable bulwark against the world's chaos and absurdity.

"I don't want
to reincarnate back
into an Earth that has
thirty billion people that
pretty much all live in
small cages like those
poor people of
Hong Kong."

Alex Chiu

ALEX CHIU is immortal, unless he dies because of an accident or murder. He sells immortality rings, which he claims on his website are the "most important invention in human history." He also sells Georgouspil.

Although you sell a few products, I imagine the one that sells the most is your Immortality Ring. Can you tell me a little bit about how it works? Does it actually make you immortal or does it just make you totally hot forever?

Actually I only sell what I invented plus a book I wrote. I sell the Immortality Rings, the Gorgeouspil powder, and my Super I-Ching book. The two magnetic rings on your small fingers function as a turbine which increases the whole body's chi flow, thus increasing healing process. So you heal faster than you age. Therefore, you stay young forever.

This invention cannot protect you from accidents or murder.

After you wear the rings, your body heals faster than it ages. The rings do protect you from most illnesses and diseases. So it would be harder for a person to get cancer or ulcer, etc.

What about the GorgeousPil? You say using it will help reach physical perfection. What does that mean to you?

The Immortality Rings themselves will increase your body's healing. But it's just not enough to cure handicaps or deformation of your body. So this is where Gorgeouspil came from.

On your website you talk about your philosophy about the future. Can you tell me a little bit about what you think will go down?

First, I actually want a one-world government which will enforce population control. So in the future you need to apply for a license in order to have a baby. The government will check the world's capacity rate, which should be 500 million people in the whole world. If the world has more than 500 million people, then nobody is permitted to have kids. Special permission could be granted occasionally to people with special privilege. I understand some would argue if nobody is allowed to have kids then this world will be full of senior citizens. Then who has the energy to work? Not so if everybody wears my rings. If you wear the rings, you don't age, remember?

Second, I believe that there should be a limit on how much a person can earn. Every time a multimillionaire or a billionaire is created, tens of thousands of other people will become poorer. So money is not unlimited. Money is sort of like a swimming pool. If there is a giant monster that can suck up half of the water in a pool in one gulp, then there will be less water for everybody else to drink. So I think if we have a world government, we can set a cap on how much a person can earn.

Let's say once you earned $75 million dollars, you need to quit what you are doing and sell your company to somebody else. I mean, seriously, $75 million is a lot of money. Who needs that kind of money to survive?

Third, the one-world government should enforce a very strict law to protect wild life and nature. We have to force everybody to recycle. We have to enforce a stricter recycling habit, like all Styrofoam must be crushed and reused and cannot be dumped into landfills. Ban cruelty to animals and stop people from selling fur or bear bile, etc.

Basically I know that there is reincarnation. I know nobody can truly live forever because one day something will happen to you and you will simply wait to be reincarnated and come back to Earth. I want to keep this Earth clean so the next time I come I will have a pleasant and easy life. I don't want to reincarnate back into an Earth that has thirty billion people that pretty much all live in small cages like those poor people of Hong Kong.

You say on your website "Alicia Silverstone is so beautiful. She is the example of a perfect human blend. I shall endeavor to make everyone as beautiful as Alicia with my inventions. My inventions are to help people reach perfection." Do you still consider her the perfect woman?
I basically don't touch my website very much. I wrote that almost twenty years ago. But I keep it up there because I am a loyal guy and plus very traditional. I like to keep my website old school. But yeah she is still very pretty.

You mentioned to me that you were arrested in 2010 and were on probation for three years. What was up with that?
In 2009, the postal police raided my house with a search warrant. Then in 2010 they charged me with ten federal felonies for six refunds that I did not issue. I must admit some of these refunds that I did not honor was my fault. I was offended when customers sent back the rings or foot braces claiming

that I am a fraud, claiming that these rings cannot give them immortality. I was extremely insulted any time customers sent back the rings with an insulting note. So sometimes I just kept their money. But I got into trouble for that. So I got arrested, plead guilty, got fined $10,000 and three years' probation.

Basically this is a very tough field. Everybody picks on people who are in alternative medicine. Most people think alternative medicine is a huge fraud. Small guys like me can never receive an FDA approval because each approval from beginning to finish would cost nearly thirty million dollars and would take many years. Only huge drug companies can apply for an FDA approval. And most people think if you are not approved by the FDA and not recommended by doctors, then you are a fraud.

I have high school kids calling me all the time to mock me. What I hate the most about this business is to hear young people, fourteen- to twenty-some-years-old, mocking me for creating an amazing and useful invention. These kids are even more close-minded than their grandpas. Which really makes me very sad and disgusted.

And just a year ago they sent Kevin Trudeau to prison again. Now he is serving ten years behind bars, all for writing a book teaching people how to lose weight. When I was arrested I told myself, I don't want to end up like Kevin Trudeau, getting fined $38 million dollars by the FCC and get tossed in prison for ten years. So recently, I began maintaining a very low profile. I no longer promote my website. Because I fear if I became too famous again, then these people will be after me again.

"...I once talked to a fetish model that told me that necro, or sleep stuff was some of the easiest money she could make, being that all she did was just lie there."

Dixie Comet

DIXIE COMET is a fetish model. If you like eating cake off chicks' asses, banging passed out women, or for pretty much anything else you can think of, check her out. The odds are she has done a video about what you are into and she does custom video work.

How long have you been in the business and how did you get started?

I have been in the business since 2009. I started out web camming to get comfortable with performing for an audience. Shortly thereafter I started shooting a little bit of hardcore porn in Los Angeles. Then a couple of months later, I dove into the fetish porn world and found my true love and a kinky side that I didn't even know I had. It's sad it took me twenty-six years to find my kinky self.

There are tons of fetishes out there, some of the more popular to do with feet, mind control, FemDom and stuff like that. What are some of the more odd things that you have been asked to do?

Oh boy! I love this question. I've definitely been asked to get drunk and stoned in the morning while wearing a silk kimono and booty shorts. I was instructed to piss the booty shorts, play in the pee puddle, then twerk in my booty shorts. That one never came to fruition.

I have also been asked to buy a conversion van and go on a road trip with a couple of girlfriends. While on the road trip, us gals were to smoke cigarettes and cigars and burn holes all over the interior-along with pissing all over the inside of the van. Then when we were done destroying the inside, the dude requested that we blow up the van in the desert. Like big explosion and a fireball. I can't make this shit up. This also never came to fruition.

I once played a mom who was in an abusive marriage—the mom was forced to hold her pee by her off-screen husband while she got all of her chores done in the kitchen. The camera was from the perspective of a small child who was watching the story unfold. The mom is desperate to pee and keeps asking her husband to be excused but he keeps telling her no. Eventually she ends up pissing herself in front of the kid and as she is pissing herself she is crying in humility and is apologizing to her kid.

These are all pee-centric but totally bizarre... in a good way. I've shot sweater fetish—where you are dressed head to toe in sweaters and then have sex or get tied up. I've been covered in gold paint and transformed into a statue. I have a frequent customer who loves to see me get my foot broken mysteriously then I hop around looking for a bandage and crutches. I've been bound and forced to watch a loop of a scene from *Gremlins* while yelling at the damsel on the TV to get out of peril—all the while having a Hitachi [power tool] tethered to me and forced to orgasm. I get a doozy at least once a week... never a dull moment!

I once talked to a fetish model that told me that necro, or sleep stuff was some of the easiest money she could make, being that all she did was just lie there.

Are there things you thought you were going to hate but ended up not minding at all?
That girl is right on the money. Sleepy stuff is totally one of my faves! To answer your question: impact and corporal. When I first started dipping my toes into BDSM I wasn't really sure if I could do the pain thing or not. I had been spanked in bondage but it wasn't done in the proper impact play protocol. Then I tried it with someone who was a total lifestyle punishment Dom and was properly warmed up and all that jazz. That's when I realized, oh shit, I'm totally a pain slut. Ok, I really don't consider myself a pain slut but I do like a good caning or spanking when there is some sexual gratification involved, e.g, the Hitachi.

When I first peed my pants, that was pretty damn gratifying. I didn't think that I was going to hate it; I was unsure if I was going to be able to do it. It's not really acceptable to piss your pants after the age of like two or whatever... so getting over that mindset and letting my bladder loose in my pants was kind of amazing. I felt like a deviant. And now I exploit my fetish and make money off of it. Win!

What are your limits? Is there anything you won't do?
I get asked to do scat all the time because I shoot a lot of pee fetish... that is a hard NO. I'm not into electro play much... I really just can't stand the smell. I won't do much anal, especially penis penetration... gotta keep something sacred for the bedroom at home. I always keep an open mind when confronted with something new. I will try anything once as long as it isn't breaking any laws or hurting anyone or anything.

So many guys, and women too, are into sexual stuff that society considers odd. How does it make you feel to be someone that brings those people what they want?

It is very gratifying. The more odd, the better... I dig weird. I love making my customers and fans happy. On a side note to this question: Think about all the death fetishists or the people who like chloroform knockouts or rape fantasy porn—we are fulfilling their fantasies and satisfying their cravings in a safe, controlled environment for their viewing pleasure. I'd like to think that entertaining those fantasies keeps the majority from actually going out committing possible felonies. We are doing society a huge favor.

"If Kaczynski's actions ultimately have some effect on averting technological disaster, there will be no doubt: his actions were justified."

David Skrbina

DAVID SKRBINA is a professor of philosophy at the University of Michigan, who at one point got kind of tight with Ted Kaczynski, who is more commonly known as the Unabomber, and in fact wrote a forward to one of his books. Obviously he is not a big fan of technology. Skrbina's latest book is *The Metaphysics of Technology*.

Can you tell me a bit about how you and Kaczynski began to communicate? Are you still in touch with him today?

Back in 2003, I began work on a new course at the University of Michigan: 'Philosophy of Technology.' Surprisingly, such a course had never been offered before, at any of our campuses. I wanted to remedy that deficiency.

I then began to pull together recent and relevant material for the course, focusing on critical approaches to technology. These, to me, were more insightful and more interesting, and were notably under-analyzed among current philosophers of technology. Most of them are either neutral toward modern technology, or positively embrace it, or accept its presence resignedly. As I found out, very few philosophers of the past four decades adopted anything like a critical stance. This, for me, was highly revealing.

Anyway, I was well aware of Kaczynski's manifesto, "Industrial society and its future," which was published in late 1995 at the height of the Unabomber mania. I was very impressed with its analysis, even though most of the ideas were not new to me (many were reiterations of arguments by Jacques Ellul, for example—see his 1964 book, *The Technological Society*). But the manifesto was clear and concise, and made a compelling argument.

After Kaczynski was arrested in 1996, and after a year-long trial process, he was stashed away in a super-max prison in Colorado. The media then decided that, in essence, the story was over. Case closed. No need to cover Kaczynski or his troubling ideas ever again.

By 2003, I suspected he was still actively researching and writing, but I had heard nothing of substance about him in years. So I decided to write to him personally, hoping to get some follow-up material that might be useful in my new course. Fortunately, he replied. That began a long string of letters, all on the problem of technology. To date, I've received something over 100 letters from him.

Most of the letters occurred in the few years prior to, and just after, the publication of *Technological Slavery*. Several of his more important and detailed replies to me were included in that book—about 100 pages worth. We've had less occasion to communicate in the past couple years. My most recent letter from him was in late 2014.

You have said that his ideas "threaten to undermine the power structure of our technological order. And since the system's defenders are unable to defeat the ideas, they choose to attack the man who wrote them." Can you expand on that?

The present military and economic power of the U.S. government, and governments everywhere, rests on advanced technology. Governments, by their very nature, function to manipulate and coerce people—both their own citizens, and any other non-citizens whom they declare to be of interest. Governments have a monopoly on force, and this force is manifest through technological structures and systems.

Therefore, all governments—and in fact anyone who would seek to exert power in the world—must embrace modern technology. American government, at all levels, is deeply pro-tech. So too are our corporations, universities, and other organized institutions. Technology is literally their life-blood. They couldn't oppose it in any substantial way without committing virtual suicide.

So, when a Ted Kaczynski comes along and reminds everyone of the inherent and potentially catastrophic problems involved with modern technology, "the system" doesn't want you to hear it. It will do everything possible to distort or censor such discussion. As you may recall, during the final years of the Unabomber episode, there was very little—astonishingly little—discussion of the actual ideas of the manifesto. Now and then, little passages would be quoted in the newspapers, but that was it; no follow-up, no discussion, no analysis.

Basically, the system's defenders had no counterarguments. The data, empirical observation, and commonsense—all were on the side of Kaczynski. There was no rational case to be made against him.

The only option for the defenders was an ad hominem attack: to portray Kaczynski as a sick murderer, a crazed loner, and so on. That was the only way to 'discredit' his ideas. Of course, as we know, the ad hominem tactic is a logical fallacy. Kaczynski's personal situation, his mental state, or even his extreme actions, have precisely zero bearing on the strength of his arguments.

The system's biggest fear was—and still is—that people will believe that he was right. People might begin, in ways small or large, to withdraw from, or to undermine, the technological basis of society. This cuts to the heart of the system. It poses a fundamental threat, to which the system has few options, apart from on-going propaganda efforts, or brute force.

What do you think of the fact that when our government, or any figure in authority such as a police officer, kills in the name of the established belief system, it is thought of as just. But when a guy like Kaczynski kills in the name of his belief system, he is thought of as a deranged psychopath?
As I mentioned, governmental authorities have a monopoly on force. Whenever they use it, it is, almost by definition, 'right.' Granted, police can be convicted of 'excessive force.' But such cases, as we know, are very rare. And militaries can never be so convicted.

At best, if the public is truly appalled by some lethal action of our police or military, they may vote in a more 'pacifist' administration. But even that rarely works. People were disgusted by the warmonger George W. Bush, and so they voted in the "antiwar" Obama. Ironically, he continued on with much the same killing. And through foreign aid and UN votes, Obama continues to support and defend murderous regimes around the world. So much for pacifism.

Let's keep in mind: Kaczynski killed three people. This was tragic and regrettable, but still, it was 'just' three people. American police kill that many citizens every other day, on average. The same with Obama's drone operators. Technology kills many times that number, every day—even every hour. Let's keep things in perspective.

Kaczynski killed in order to gain the notoriety necessary to get the manifesto into the public eye. And it worked. When it was published, the *Washington Post* sold something like 1.2 million copies that day—still a record. He devised a plan, executed it, and thereby caused millions of people to contemplate the problem of technology in a way they never had before.

Does the end justify the means? It's too early to tell. If Kaczynski's actions ultimately have some effect on averting technological disaster, there will be no doubt: his actions were justified. They may yet save millions of lives, not to mention much of the natural world. Time will tell.

How has your experience communicating with Kaczynski changed you as a person and as a philosopher?
As a philosopher, not that much. Kaczynski generally avoids philosophy and metaphysics, preferring practical issues. In a sense, we are operating on different planes, even as we are working on the same problem.

As a person, I have a greater understanding of the basis for the 'extreme' actions that he took. It's not often in life that you get a chance to communicate with someone with such a total commitment to their cause. It's impressive.

Also, the media treatment of his whole case has been enlightening. When *Technological Slavery* came out in 2010, I expected that there would be at least some media coverage. But there was none. The most famous "American terrorist" publishes a complete book from a super-max prison—and it's not news? Seriously? Compare this topic to the garbage shown on our national evening news programs, and it's a joke. National Public Radio, *60 Minutes*, *Wired* magazine, etc.—all decided it wasn't newsworthy. Very telling.

One last thing: Expect to hear from Kaczynski again soon. His second book is nearing completion. The provisional title is "Anti-Tech Revolution: Why and How." But don't look for it on your evening news.

Eric Holler

ERIC HOLLER deals in murderabilia, which basically means that he sells the writings and artifacts of murderers to collectors. He runs Serial Killers Ink, which is one of the more successful businesses of that nature.

A lot of people are going to want to know you got started in this business. What separates Serial Killers Ink from the competition?

I started writing to Richard Ramirez, the Night Stalker back in 1997. We struck up a friendship and he soon asked if I would act as his art dealer. I did. I then began writing other infamous killers and selling items for them. As far as being successful—I've always focused on my own shit not worrying about what anyone else was doing in this industry.

Can you give me some examples of the things that you guys sell? How about some of the oddest?

Artwork, craft items, and letters generally make up the true crime collectibles industry. A few of the oddest items? Bullet fragments from the body of a surviving victim of the Aurora movie theater massacre. That would be up there. Yard soil from the yard of Anthony Sowell ("The Cleveland Strangler"), where he buried his victims. Panties that belonged to Christa Pike. Santa Claus suit that belonged to John Robinson aka 'The Slave Master' that he wore to children's Christmas parties.

What are some of the highest priced items you have sold?

John Wayne Gacy paintings. Signed Ted Bundy items. A signed drawing by Ed Gein. Those all listed and sold in the four-digit range.

I like fucked up people way more than the next guy, but have you ever had to deal with someone that freaked you out?

People in line at the local Quickie mart freak me out more than serial killers do.

"When I first started writing to killers, the craziness of it all was the driving factor."

Serial killers are usually pretty cool people when you get to know them.

I have always been fascinated by abnormal psychology, and people that do things far outside of cultural norms. I also love making people feel uncomfortable and pushing limits. What makes this type of work interesting to you?

I too have always been drawn to dark or taboo things. When I first started writing to killers, the craziness of it all was the driving factor. But now, some eighteen or so years later, it's really the money that makes all this interesting to me. I still have a passion for all this crazy shit, but the money is why I still do it and is the driving factor. It's what I do...

"We must be on constant guard against even our own eyes."

John Davis

JOHN DAVIS is the President of The Flat Earth Society. I would give anything to have that business card. He has been interviewed by organizations such as the BBC and regularly is interviewed on radio and podcasts. He is in the process of writing a book about his belief system.

Let's get right down it. I know it may be hard to sum up briefly, but why do you believe the Earth is flat?

I could cite various physical phenomena and rational concrete reasons for why I believe the Earth is flat; quite likely I can do so better than the average round earther can justify his view. However, I think it's far more telling to relate how, not why, I came to believe in a flat earth.

One day while walking in the woods as a young man I had a notable experience that lead me to question everything I've taken for granted as true over the years; all those things we simply accept without properly examining their logical and rational basis and foundations. One could say, like many today, that up to this point I was standing on the shoulders of giants, but I had a deaf ear to both what they had to say about the matter as well as what assumptions they had to take to lead them to their position. This led me to a lengthy study into various ways we view the world, both orthodox and unorthodox, and their rational consequences and foundations. During this period of study and examination I came to some literature from the Flat Earth Society. Something about it just resonated with me—not only on a personal level, but also on a strictly logical level.

On another level, it seemed to me that some of the method used by this supposedly ridiculous group was far closer to the method of the aforementioned giants than what we see today from science as a whole. I remember thinking, "These are people who truly value knowledge, and they do so at a real cost—social stigma."

It is easy to believe the Earth is round—you just have to accept what everybody else is saying. It is much harder to get to the roots of why you believe what you believe and make an informed and conscious decision, especially when this decision is in discord with popular opinion; then hopefully you can grow. It's about examining the question—well what if 2+2 equaled 5? If this were to be true, what does it say, and does it yield anything fruitful?

The architect Le Corbusier once said to his students "first to look and then to observe, and finally perhaps to discover." It seemed that I was surrounded on all sides by those who have not even looked, let alone observed. How could they hope to discover? And here comes a group based on a methodology rooted deeply in looking. I have to say, it was a breath of fresh air!

Do you think that leaders who say the Earth is round are just misguided, or is it a conspiracy of sorts?

Many in our group would point to a planar conspiracy. They would cite the map the United Nations choose for their logo and various Cold War narratives to justify an Illuminati group is hiding the truth. Some even say I am a member of the Illuminati, acting as controlled opposition.

To me this seems a bit misconceived, however I can hardly discount their view in whole as it must have some worth. In general, I'd rather assume error over malice. Even if there was a conspiracy, time and time again we have seen that you can't really destroy a point of view. The worry of a group creating an alternate flat earth astronomy as Orwell warned us about is one I feel will be evened out by the tides of time. It is beyond our astronomers to create a dual astronomy—they are far too busy clutching onto their own for dear life.

We think we have the answers to almost everything. We have to do this on a very real psychological level to live our daily lives. We can't go bumbling around the world in a state of confusion or we would find ourselves not making much progress both personally and as a society—it would be quite an unpleasant way to live. Perhaps this is why we have so many mythologies across all cultures—an honest and necessary urge to know where we stand so we can then walk.

All we really have though is one angle of looking at the larger picture. I'd like to think that the leaders are simply looking at reality from a different angle than I am. And that's good. There is much use to the other angle. However, far greater use is to be found in recognizing that there are more angles. Take the early success of science by the Ancients due to the multitude of schools of thought. Even today we can note the persistence of the sacred in an age where information attempts to make everything mundane.

I am sure you are tired of this question, but if the Earth is flat, what might be on the other side?

Not at all. While it might be fun to speculate about the other side, I tend not to guess without sufficient reason. Unfortunately, all I can say is that I don't know. I haven't been there. To go further than that would be to attempt to stretch a very small tarp over a very large area with the hopes that it would not tear. You would either fail, or perhaps worse, ruin your tarp.

This is somewhat similar to what I feel many are doing in modern physics in regards to the Big Bang. Not satisfied with what they have, scientists have now taken one more step towards being a religion with the creation of their own Genesis. While it's fine to say, "this is what looks like happened", it's also quite silly to hold the Big Bang as something that is "true." A scientist has the obligation to point out the obvious (and not so obvious) flaws in his argument as well as why he believes it. If he does not do that, he's just an academic pushing a precarious point of view—essentially a used car salesman.

I agree with you that people will basically believe anything they are told. How are you planning on getting the word out?
I'm just finishing up my book on the flat earth and it should be available by the end of the year. In it, rather than attempting to change people's minds through an account piece by piece of my model, I instead focus more on aspects that will lead one to find their own view of the world.

One of the topics I talk about is our unique ability as a people to take what we are given as true—even to the point that they change how they see the world. The examples of what I call conventional sight are amazing, and one can really see them for what they are from the flat earth perspective. Of course this is by far not the only thing one can see from our perspective. From where we stand, it's hard not exclaim "Quantum Ab Hoc!"

For example, every so often I'm approached by an interested person claiming to have seen the curvature of Earth at the beach. Now note here, they are not talking about how ships recede below the horizon as they move away from us, but an actual curve to the natural horizon line itself. We can debunk this quite easily—Lynch for example in the December 2008 *Applied Optics*, writes that pilots say they can't even see curvature at altitudes of 35,000 miles.

One of our members who is a pilot confirms this and the math is fairly easy and available on sources like WolfRam and Wikipedia. While we can then explain this particular example away with perhaps the curvature of the eye itself, or some other phenomena, the far more likely explanation is that people are seeing what they want to see. This can be backed up quite easily using our current knowledge of the mind.

This should be a bit disturbing to us. It is important that we don't take what we know as true; aside from affecting our behavior, it also affects how we see the world itself! We must be on constant guard against even our own eyes.

How many members do you have at this point?

While our official member count is low, one can simply follow a hashtag on any social media network to see how much our point of view has grown. I suppose we don't care much for joining societies and getting a certificate. Those aren't really things to be valued, however they are things our society offers.

On the other hand, it is been a great disappointment to see how many have flocked to our cause based off a few celebrities agreeing with our view. That is not exactly what we like to see and it is in fact in contrast to our *raison d'être*. We don't want to convince people the Earth is flat. We already know that for ourselves. We want to convince people to question, to think, and then hopefully to solve. If they land on the flat earth—great. If not, then we are still happy; the more angles we look at reality the better for us to understand where we are and where we are going.

Does it anger you at times, that the whole "Flat Earther" thing is basically used as an insult in our society?
I wouldn't say it gets me angry—it is more of a disappointment. If we'd like to be a culture that truly values science and not just a reiteration of the dark ages (where a privileged class hands us down dogma), we need to get beyond this pigeonholed point of view where any non-coherent idea is labeled as "dangerous" by those like Neil DeGrasse Tyson. Many of the great advances of science come from ideas that seem to stand on shaky grounds at the time.

Revolutionary science looks like a flat earth. The rest is bookkeeping and puzzle solving. To deny this is what is truly dangerous. Denial might get us a microwave oven to cook our food faster, but it keeps us treading water in the river that is truth.

The time for herding and puzzle solving is over. We need to think for ourselves and take responsibility for what we believe. We have seen far too often the consequences of the opposite behavior.

Worldviews come about for a reason; their creation is based in the needs of the society around it. If there is a group around saying something that seems silly, it is saying it for a reason. It didn't just spontaneously generate—it had a cause. We really should not be running after these groups with a pitchfork, but instead we need to be asking "Why are they here?" and then perhaps "How can we solve this?" Or put more simply, "What is its desired effect?"

If we don't, we are more than likely going to persecute our age's Galileo. It is the square pegs, the outsiders, the weird, the uncomfortable, and the bogus sciences that really change how we look at things. We need to stand with Niels Bohr when he said "Not crazy enough to be true!" instead of clinging to our fragile security blanket that is our view of the world. Take the red pill. Go down the rabbit hole. Peer beyond the veil. Look behind the curtain. You might solve something of use if you just question and then think for yourself.

Jim Crawford

JIM CRAWFORD is an antinatalist. I know I already have one of those in this book, but to be honest I never expected to find even one to interview, let alone two. His latest book is *Confessions of an Antinatalist*, published by the ever brave Nine-Banded Books.

Can you tell me a bit about what antinatalism means to you and why you decided to write a book about it?

I should probably start with the second part of your question and proceed from there. I guess it was about ten years ago that I discovered the wonderful world of blogging. I'd been writing a ton of poems and posting them on various poetry websites, and blogging offered a free and easy method for archiving and sharing the material. That was about the extent of my writing for quite a while. It was a little later on that I developed an itch to express myself and my primary existential concerns outside the confines of formal poetry. I knew that the subject matter would have to tie in somehow with the problem that's increasingly plagued me since I was very young, which was the challenge of reconciling an optimistic view of life in the face of terrible suffering, human and otherwise. And here we come to the first part of your question, for in examining this dilemma with ever increasing emotional urgency for most of my adult life I had already come to the rather depressing conclusion that no honest reconciliation was possible. It seemed that I'd already run the gamut of religious possibilities, as well as those of more generalized philosophical and psychological coping strategies, but nothing had stuck.

After several decades of searching for some kind of justification for the way human beings have always done things, and finding none, I finally and fully acquiesced to the truth that I'd known from the beginning, a truth that had been gnawing at my guts since I could remember. The truth that life should never have been, and that the only human endeavor ultimately worth its own weight should be directed toward the alleviation of suffering and death by striking at its very root, sentient existence itself. Notable futurist Nick Bostrom penned an essay several years back entitled "The Fable of the Dragon-Tyrant." In it, he explores what he

"I just don't want you to have children, because of the very real possibility that somewhere down the lifeline they might become NOT happy, and none of us want that, do we?"

sees as the predicament of human suffering and death embodied in the form of a gluttonous monster who demands the sacrifice of thousands of men, women and children on a daily basis for its own eventual consumption. The gist of Bostrom's allegory is that humanity as a whole should be directing its efforts towards killing the dragon; indeed, that there is a primary moral imperative to do so and as quickly as possible, seeing that each day delayed adds another stratum to an already unconscionably cumulative body count. Of course, there are two ways to kill a dragon. One way is to fire missiles at the thing, keeping our fingers crossed for a true and mortal strike. This is the approach taken by Bostrom in his treatise. I see a few problems with this proposed method of dragon slaying, namely: (1) We don't know that our dragon-tyrant can be killed in this manner. All we do know is that he's been with us forever, and that just when we think we're getting a handle on taming him, he explodes up out of the earth to ravage and plunder us once again, sometimes in new and even more virulent ways. (2) We have no idea of whether or not a slain dragon remains dead forever, or if in fact the slain dragon has relatives who might sooner or later show up seeking revenge. Nor is it possible, without some kind of wizardly foreknowledge to know if this is the case. In fact, I've heard rumors that there's another beast, the granddaddy of all dragons, lurking outside the limits of our observational horizon who is even now eating away at the fundamental fabric of our existence. His name is Entropy, the defiler of all our dreams. In this sense only those of us with the least humility dare to sit at the victory banquet table without at least sometimes casting uneasy looks over our collective shoulder. (3) Even if we grant that the dragon-tyrant can be killed, at least in the context of temporal existence and momentarily disregarding the long term aspects of universal disintegration whose diminishing animative energies we are only borrowing for a relatively short while, we're still faced with the problem of 'how long?,' and its concomitant sixty-four dollar question, 'how many?' What's it worth in terms of body bags on our march toward the end of our proposed existential rainbow? Does our aggregate hope of eventual quasi-immortality for the species justify the costs, the generation of generations of steppingstones toward an imagined Nirvana contrived of flesh and blood and love and loss?

Where's the payday to all those who suffer for the dreams of some hypothetical progeny who may or may not ever exist? Who gave their permission to be exploited in this fashion? Certainly not I, nor my children, or anyone else for that matter. Apparently our basic ethical principles are valid only insomuch as they exist to further our vicarious immortality fantasies. Beyond that, it seems like the only sure remedy available for those who resent being forced into a situation they never asked for is suicide. A stinging balm, to be sure, and at least as acrid as the dragon's breath. On the other hand, there's another way to kill a dragon, and that is simply to stop feeding it. More precisely, the idea is to stop growing the crops that the dragon thrives upon. Take away the fuel and the dragon starves, and THAT is what antinatalism means to me. Antinatalism is a means to an end, that end being the surcease of suffering and death on this planet. Well, not ALL suffering and death, granted. There's that whole 'circle of life' thing to be considered, what with humanity being only one of billions of life forms on Earth. Nevertheless it's a start, and there are practical approaches that could be implemented such that human misery and death could be abolished in a single generation, simply by putting the kibosh on the whole procreation thing. It's very easy not to have a baby, after all. People do it all the time. Or don't do it, as the case may be. And when that last person falls, it will be in recognition that the dragon was us all along. Anyway, to finish up with the second part of your question, I did some Internet searching along the lines of 'the morality of procreation.' Somewhere along the way I discovered the term 'antinatalism' which seemed to make nutshell sense to me, so I filched it and named my new blog Antinatalism—The Greatest Taboo. Shortly thereafter I discovered another blogger named Chip Smith who had written some articles about the subject. Chip also happened to be the owner and operator of his own publishing house, namely Nine Banded Books specializing in, shall we say, somewhat controversial subject matter. I decided to contact him, some correspondence flared up between us and before you know it I was a published author. I'll always be grateful for the opportunity he afforded me to express myself. Who'd have thunk?

Why do you think people believe life is so important?
This question sort of presupposes that people approach this subject as a logical proposition, but I just don't believe that's true in most (and arguably all) cases. There's a temptation to go off on a myriad of tangents here regarding beliefs and motivations. To avoid doing that (since this isn't MY book, after all), I'm going to restrict my answer to what I hope is a concise and baseline response. Biological organisms in the main simply DO NOT WANT TO DIE.

It goes against our evolutionary heritage, our programming. The urge to survive is a basic feature of evolution. Naturally, when I speak of evolutionary 'urges' I'm not saying that amoebas kneel in fear and trembling before the throne of the Primary One Celled Organism lest they be smoten (smited?). What I AM saying is that the fundamental responses and reflexes innate in the lower organisms have their correlates in human behavior, and EVEN in the abstract processes of higher thinking, and therein lies the rub. If someone swings their fist at you, you may react by merely ducking your head, or perhaps by raising your own arm and blocking the punch. You might even return the sentiment in kind. But what do you do when that fist is made of the abstract flesh and knuckle of thirty-year mortgages, or decline of job satisfaction, or the knowledge that you have a genetic predisposition towards intestinal cancer, or that if the rain doesn't come you're going to lose your crop and you and your family are going to starve? How do you block or dodge that kind of blow? One way we have of reacting to all this is to fight back in the same kind of complicated and convoluted way that the attacks come at us. To deal with the mortgage we invest much of our time and energy in earning money. When we discover that we hate our jobs (as most of us do), we distract ourselves with television, alcohol, drugs, and the variety of minutia that serve as a hiding place to protect ourselves from our own psychic misery. When faced with imminent doom in the guise of disease or environmental hardships we run for help from friends and neighbors, from the government, and as a last resort from the skies themselves (God knows I'm good!). However, at the end of the day and no matter how valiantly we have fought back the tides of corruption and injustice, we know that we are finite creatures, and that we are bound to die. We have found the enemy and the enemy is time, and there's nothing in our power that can help us stand against our final, irrevocable dissolution, while none of our evolutionarily honed defense mechanisms make a damned bit of difference in the end. This knowledge is what sets us against other living things. It is our curse.

But do you think our aforementioned evolutionary-fueled response mechanisms are going to knuckle under to THAT particular bully of inevitability? Hell no! And so human ingenuity plays its trump card.

Since time seems to be the primary agent of our ontological sorrows, we simply cast it away with a flick of our abstract wrists and embrace timelessness. Eternity. We set our 'true' natures outside the restrictions of change and decay.

Of course, God goes by many names. One of those names is 'Meaning', or to line my answer up with your question a little bit better, 'Importance'. Either way, what we're talking about here is the creation of an ontological object built of purely abstract stuff, stored away in a forever enduring treasure chest beyond the reach of thieves, where neither moth nor rust corrupt. This objectification of our yearning for timelessness is then folded back into the stream of temporal existence as a totem, an embodiment of eternity in finitude. No need for a literal one-to-one correspondence here, although depending on the sophistication of the cultural inflection involved you might get some of that.

Or a lot. The main thing to remember is that these abstract structures are all built in the service of fooling ourselves into believing that we can duck a punch thrown by the universe. For the modern existential pugilist who can't quite make himself believe that a literal God is in his corner, thus providing him with a distinct, personal immortality—in other words, he is unable to translate the totemic promises back into an intellectually satisfying personal eternity gambit—he is stuck with trying to make the best of what he has. An abstract object of ungrounded hopefulness grafted onto the continued survival of the species.

In summation, why do people believe that life is important? Precisely because it is not. But the truth hurts like a punch in the face, the punches keep coming, and all we can do is throw up our invisible hands and pretend the raining blows are divine kisses.

Your blog has a lot of angry comments from people about your views. What angers and terrifies people so much about antinatalism?
Again, for the person who has invested his own sense of immortality in the immortality of the species as a whole down through time, to posit the end of the species is to directly threaten that person's life. Fear and anger are tied directly into the survival mechanisms, our fight-or-flight responses.

Some years back on my blog, I coined a term (I THINK I coined it, anyway); namely, 'vicarious immortality'. I think it pretty much speaks for itself. We know we're going to die. We don't want to die, in the sense of irrevocable personal annihilation, anyway. So we fake ourselves out. We tell ourselves in a sort of subtextual way that as long as the species survives, so do we.

I related in my book the story of my then young daughter's reaction to the imminent 'putting down' of a family pet. When I tried to explain to her that everything dies, her response back to me was basically "Then what's the point?". Now, this really wasn't a purely philosophical question at all. In fact, it was a mostly visceral reaction in the face of a feeling of utter futility, a reaction that I think most of us can empathize with. At such moments the realization of our own danger quickens within us. The truth of our situation breaks through the veneer of cultural conditioning put in place to protect us from situations just like this, and we find ourselves feeling threatened and attacked by a force against which we cannot defend ourselves, other than by retreating back behind the veil that only partially obscures the truth of ourselves from ourselves. It's a horrible knowledge, and it's understandable that the more intractable among us might lash out in anger at the messenger of such dire forebodings. Not a reaction I relish, but I get it.

I actually enjoy my life, but I also don't really care if I die tomorrow. Does that make me an argument for or against your views?
Neither. Stated as succinctly as I can, antinatalism is the ethical position that we shouldn't be bringing new lives into the world due to the risk of unacceptable suffering and inevitable death. At least that's my approach to the thing. There are other issues at stake as well, such as the question of consent, but that's something I don't spend much time worrying over. To be honest, if suffering was completely taken off the table I doubt I'd find the emotional wherewithal inside myself to even bother making a fuss about the subject, though other antinatalists might surely disagree. Personally, I am very happy that you are happy, and I hope you continue to be happy until the end of your days. I just don't want you to have children, because of the very real possibility that somewhere down the lifeline they might become NOT happy, and none of us want that, do we?

Jamal Joseph

JAMAL JOSEPH is a former Black Panther who served time in prison for hiding Black Panther fugitives from the FBI. He is now an author, a poet, and a professor at Columbia University. He also is probably the nicest man that agreed to let me interview him. His book *Panther Baby* is published by Algonquin Books.

Where were you, mentally, emotionally and spiritually, when you joined the Black Panther Party as a fifteen-year-old?

I was a smart, respectful kid being raised by an adopted grandmother who had a sixth grade education but very aware of civil rights and social justice. Her parents had been slaves. Growing up in the south she saw family members beat and lynched. My grandmother worked as a maid and was active in the church. Her hope for me was college and to become a doctor or a lawyer. I was an honor student and belong to teen leadership clubs but also played ball and hung out with the rough guys trying to figure out how to be a man. I had been smacked around by enough cops and been called "nigger" enough time to know that blackmanhood would be a challenge—if not a war—and that education and an upper mobile job would not make things right. Maybe I would be better—but my community and people would not. The sense of racial pride I got from grandma, those teen groups and the local church and community center gave me a sense that the world was bigger than me and that somehow I needed to help change it. Walking into the Panther Office filled me pride, awe, and a sense that I had found a place where I could be that strong man and a change agent. The Panthers were strong, brilliant, filled with love for the community, politically conscious and without question—badassed!

How much of the "scary" and "violent" reputation of the Black Panther Party, and the Black Liberation Army (BLA), was deserved, and how much of it was a fabrication of the government and people in power?

My friends told me that the Panthers would give me a gun and make me go out and kill a white dude to prove myself when I joined. Instead I was given a

"The two biggest myths of the Panthers were that we hated white people and that we advocated violence."

stack of books including Malcolm X and Frantz Fanon and taught the meaning of class struggle and socialism. The Panthers believed in armed self-defense against police brutality and military oppression. But Panthers held guns 5% of the time and babies, books, food for the community, medicine for the sick and steady hands for the elderly 95% of the time. The two biggest myths of the Panthers were that we hated white people and that we advocated violence.

How did prison change you?
An old timer gave me a life-changing lesson when I first got to prison. He said, "young brother—you can serve this time or this time serve you." I read every book in sight, I earned two college degrees via a special program that allowed a professor from University of Kansas to teach classes, I began writing poetry and plays and started a theater company that broke down racial barriers among the prisoners. What I learned in prison became the foundation for all the work I have done in the thirty years I have been out of prison—I am still a revolutionary but the weapons are arts, education and youth mentoring.

I tried to get in touch with the New Black Panther Party for an interview to no avail. Do you have an opinion on what they are doing as an organization? The New Black Liberation Militia is in theory an offshoot of the BLA.
What's missing from the offshoots and name bearers of the Panther legacy are the two things that made the Panther Party unique. The ideology of class struggle and socialism and the community programs. The Panthers made it clear that All Power to the people meant power to all oppressed people, black, white, brown, red, yellow, gay, woman, immigrant, impoverished. The Panthers built progressive coalitions that brought all groups together including and especially the antiwar movement to create and work for broad platforms for change and social justice. Panther programs like the free breakfast program, community clinics and liberation school became models for social program that exist to this day. If I just see a group yelling at a press conference or a rally but don't see them doing day to day social action work in the community then I know they are not really honoring the legacy or the lessons of the Black Panther Party.

How do you nurture your inner dissident at this point in your life?
Whether at Columbia, at the youth arts program I co-founded Impact Repertory Theater, lecturing or doing creative work I try to get people to think critically and to think with love. The greatest lesson we learned in the Panthers—and any Panther will (I guarantee) answer this question the same way—that what we taught to believe above all other things was to have "an undying love for the people." If you give people the tools to think critically from a place of love, then 99.5% of the time they will wind up in a place of healing, transformation and liberation.

"Yes, it is true that George King was the only one in the society that could receive the telepathic and channeled transmissions from the Cosmic Masters (who were extraterrestrial in nature)."

Oscar Leon

Reverend OSCAR LEON is one of the leaders of The Aetherius Society. an international spiritual organization founded by George King and dedicated to spreading, and acting upon, the teachings of advanced extraterrestrial intelligences.

Can you tell me a bit of how the Aetherius Society got started? The Aetherius Society essentially started with George King, who we refer to as Dr. George King or His Eminence Sir George King (he received various awarded doctorates, and was a consecrated archbishop). Born into a family of psychics and mediums, he developed these latent abilities within himself from an early age and studied supernatural and occult phenomena for many years. After serving in the Fire Brigade in WWII he sought out greater truths and deeper meaning and so turned his attention to the science of yoga. After almost a decade of training his mind, body and subtle senses in this science, for up to ten hours per day, he became a Master of Yoga and was able to enter into some of the highest states of consciousness known to man. With his mediumistic and yogic abilities, he started a Healing Circle whose focus was to bring forth information from the higher mental realms of Earth in order to give greater healing to those around them.

However, soon after in 1954, he received a telepathic communication, which stated, "Prepare yourself. You are to become the voice on Interplanetary Parliament". The being who communicated to Dr. King was a Master from Venus known under the pseudonym of "Aetherius". This initiated a series of Cosmic Transmissions from various Cosmic Masters, who were interplanetary and extraterrestrial in origin, which lasted several decades. The transmissions were delivered through Dr. King while he was in a state of deep meditative trance.

The Aetherius Society was initially founded by Dr. King in order to record and disseminate throughout the world these Cosmic Transmissions, which were of vital importance to the world. The messages varied in nature, but two of the main topics were (1) the dangers of nuclear experimentation and the strong advice against its use, and (2) that we should turn back to the spiritual teachings of the great Cosmic Masters who have come to our world in the past, Masters such as Jesus, Buddha, Krishna, Lao Tze, and others. The Cosmic Masters imparted great, universal spiritual teaching, though did so in a manner that could be easily understood.

The Aetherius Society soon went on to take another role, and that was in the active cooperation with these communicating Cosmic Masters in various energy manipulations for global peace and enlightenment. These are known as Cosmic Missions and most of them are still continued to this day. The primary aim of the Cosmic Missions is to radiate higher vibratory energies to the world as a whole in order to bring about world healing and enlightenment, greater balance in our ecosystem, and improve the karma of the human race.

How have things gone since the passing of your founder George King? I have read he was the only person in the society that could receive mental transmissions from aliens?
Yes, it is true that George King was the only one in the society that could receive the telepathic and channeled transmissions from the Cosmic Masters (who were extraterrestrial in nature). Before his passing he set up the administration and organization of The Aetherius Society so that it would be able to fully function long into the future after his passing. This included pre-arranged dates and times for active cooperation with the Cosmic Masters in various world-healing missions. It has been almost twenty years since his passing and The Aetherius Society is continuing strong with the performance of the Cosmic Missions that Dr. King left in its care and custody. The society has also been continuing and increasing the dissemination of the Teachings of the Cosmic Masters, as well as those given by Dr. King himself. We have added new official centers throughout the world, and our worldwide membership has increased since Dr. King passed on in 1997.

Could you tell me a bit about the spiritual energy crisis?
There are many energy shortages and crises around the world today. However, those are the physical outer manifestations, or symptoms, of a deeper energy crisis—the cause of all the outer crises. It is the Spiritual energy crisis. It's not that there is a lack of Spiritual energy available to us—in fact, our supplies are limitless—the crisis is that we do not use the Spiritual energies enough. Once we put Spiritual energy back in its rightful place, using it through prayer, healing, service and various other spiritual means, all the other energy crises will naturally correct themselves. Until we use Spiritual energy correctly and solve the Spiritual energy crisis, no matter what inventions the human race comes up they will still run short of physical energy.

How many adherents do you have throughout the world, and is this something you are interested in spreading or are you happy with a core group?

We would estimate it to be in the low thousands. Our aim is to spread the Cosmic Teachings throughout the world and to continue to perform the Cosmic Missions to our fullest capacity, as laid out by Dr. King. We are certainly interested in receiving more help in achieving these aims, for the more help we get, the more we can do for the world. However, we do not proselytize or recruit members to our organization. To join as a member is a personal choice left to each person to decide.

What will happen when the next Master from space arrives?

The implication of his coming is a time of major crisis for the world. Our understanding is that he will come openly for all people to observe. He will approach the world leaders and demonstrate to them his extraterrestrial abilities. By his presence and demonstration he will not only give an indication of his awesome power and ability, but also of how humanity has to change. As such, it is regarded as a time of the "sorting of the wheat from the chaff," between those who are ready to live as we have been taught by previous Spiritual Masters and enter in a new age upon this Earth, and those who reject this and continue to live selfishly.

Those who reject this greater Spiritual message will be reborn upon another world. Those who remain will help to create a much more enlightened planet of a higher vibration, as has been prophesied throughout the centuries.

"I got off on
the idea that they
would have a day
or two of anxiety.
It was not a real
victory, but it was
a consolation
prize."

Joshua Shea

JOSHUA SHEA was kind of a big deal in Lewiston, Maine. He was a
city councilor, ran a popular magazine, and put on a successful film
festival. He was a bonafide local celebrity. A few years back he was
arrested on sexual computer crimes and sentenced to nine months
in county jail for the crime of manipulating women on-line into
masturbating for their webcams, one of whom had not reached the
age of eighteen. Shea is working on a memoir about his rise and fall.

How did you get started manipulating women on the Internet?
I have a porn addiction, and like any addiction it can escalate before
you realize you are even sick. I was surfing for porn and I found a
couple of amateur clips that I liked. This led me to another site which was kind
of a chatroom, where you could meet a woman on line through a video camera.
It was as much about getting off on manipulation as it was sexual. Obviously, I
have power and control issues.

What sort of techniques did you use to reel women in?
After some experimentation I realized that women would not stop and talk to
someone who looked like me. The premise of the site I used is simple: the site
connects two computers via web cam to each other. If you don't like what you
see you click "next" and someone new pops up; they can do the same to you.

After being on the site for a while I realized a few of the men who repeatedly
popped up were actually just videos of good looking guys which often showed
them masturbating at the end. I figured out how to bypass my webcam and
just run a video. No one ever saw my face this way, I only typed, never spoke.
Women thought I was in my early twenties, not late thirties. I found women
always ask a guy to wave or to give the peace sign to show they are real.
They also want to see abs. Abs are to girls what boobs are to guys. If I could
get a girl to start taking her clothes off I would need to have the person on the
video do something. I went through fifty or so potential videos until I found one
that met every criteria. I was able to edit it and isolate the wave into two small

videos. Then I was able to isolate the thirty seconds he showed abs, and the two minutes he showed his penis and masturbated. Then of course was the basic eight-minute clip I would loop of the guy just typing and smiling.

Since I am a writer, good at improv and a master at manipulation, I developed a character for the video, with a long back story. He was always in California or Florida, and always from New York. I would change facts based on what the person was saying, tailoring the message to what I thought they would be most receptive to.

As an additional layer I would take seemingly pointless facts shared by the woman to do a background search. While the chat was going on over twenty minutes I would often find out their name, where they went to college and where they worked, and use that to find them on Facebook. It is easy to figure out what to say at that point to make them feel comfortable. If they played soccer in high school, I played it in college, that type of thing.

Half the girls did the "wave to show you are real" routine. Once they were comfortable and I did it enough times I could tell in five minutes if they were someone I could manipulate and convince to take her clothes off. You never come out and ask, "can I see your boobs?" you work up to it. For instance you mention she is pretty a few times but don't dwell on it. At some point you mention how you are trying to get in better shape, and she will usually make a comment about how you look like you are in good shape. Then you say something like, "I was a fat kid in high school, everyone made fun of me, but I worked hard to get where I am. Girls say they like my eyes, my lips, my chest, my abs, and as silly as this sounds, my penis." I never called it a cock until they did. It was all about following their lead after the "fat kid" speech.

Nine out of ten times they would ask to see my abs after the "fat kid" speech. I would play it shy a few times and say no, but then at some point say if I had to be topless then they had to be. One in three would ditch me at this point, I had them on the hook then I lost them. One in three would hesitate, and one in three would say okay. When I heard that I knew the hard work was over. Even if she hesitated I didn't give up. She didn't "next" me, she was still interested—slow down and try a different route.

Now this is the first illegal part. I would take video of the screen without them knowing. I would start filming first right before they were about to take their clothes off. The video was my trophy. Later I didn't use them for sexual gratification purposes, I would look at them if I was down and needed to feel a sense of accomplishment even though it was sexual exploitation. Many called me sick, I was sick, but not just sexually. In a personal and professional life that was crumbling, I didn't need to do this for sexual gratification, I needed to do it because it was the last thing I was good at. The videos filled the void once filled by all the trophies in my office.

How often were you doing this, meaning messing around on the net with women?
I did this for five or six months, it started slow, like an hour a week, then went to three times a week, then I did it every day, I think by the end of it I had about seventy-five conversations that turned sexual. True success was getting them to masturbate, which happened about twenty times.

When you totally had them on the hook, what would you get them to do?
As much as I could, if I spent two hours to see an ass it was a total waste. It meant I had read the woman wrong and was disappointed in myself. If I wanted to get her back for not showing anything or being mean to me I would fuck with her head. I would use the information my search gathered and pretend to be a friend of her dad's, or fast forward the video to show that I had conned her. Then I would click "next". I got off on the idea that they would have a day or two of anxiety. It was not a real victory, but it was a consolation prize.

How bad do you feel about doing this type of thing, and how did you get caught?
I feel very bad, it was the stupidest most depraved thing I have ever done. As to how I got caught, I am still not sure, nor do I want to know the exact details, just in case it involves somebody who is in my life. Based on the discovery in my case, I think it had to do with the underage girl, it sounds like I was not her only voyeur, she looked of age, but I was usually so drunk and exhausted when I did this, I don't know if it even would have mattered if she said she wasn't eighteen. Now if I were not caught by the police what would have happened? I don't know.

I learned a few things about women through this. They are as nuts about looks as men, even if they pretend otherwise. They see what they want, even on an eight-minute video looping for two hours. The older the woman, the more they want to get naked. They are not healthy. They all seemed depressed. Healthy people don't use a site like that. Then again, I wasn't healthy.

I could take the point of view that I never made anyone do anything. Everything they did was by choice. The flip side is we were both sick and I hurt them worse than they hurt me. I think it showed there is something very wrong with me and I have been working and will continue to work in therapy to learn what led me to this heinous decision making. Writing about it has been an eye-opening experience, it is a cautionary tale most people never think about. I just wish I wasn't made the example, although it may have saved my life.

Acknowledgments

I would be remiss if I did not thank each person in this book for allowing me to interview them. I have much respect for each of you.

I also should think Heather Payson for the friendship, Lizzy Garnatz for the support, and Patrick Quinlan for the inspiration.

The interviews with Mike Scott, Patrick Quinlan, John Zerzan, Kristian Williams, John Marmyz, David Skrbina and Alex Chiu first appeared in Disinfo.com. Marcie Gainer, thanks for publishing them.

The interview with John Davis first appeared in *Paste Magazine*.

Index of interviewees

A HEADPRESS BOOK
First published by Headpress in 2017

[email] headoffice@headpress.com
[web] www.worldheadpress.com

SUBVERSIVE
Interviews with Radicals

Text copyright © Brian Whitney
This volume copyright © Headpress 2017
Cover, book design & layout: Mark Critchell
<mark.critchell@googlemail.com>

A CIP catalogue record for this book is
available from the British Library

978-1-909394-54-4   ISBN PAPERBACK
978-1-909394-55-1   ISBN EBOOK
HARDBACK   NO-ISBN

1 H E A D P R E S S Est 1991

WWW.WORLDHEADPRESS.COM
the gospel according to unpopular culture
Special editions of this and other books are
available exclusively from Headpress

CPSIA information can be obtained
at www.ICGtesting.com
Printed in the USA
FSOW02n0213161117
41039FS